Psychology A2

The Mini Companion

Mike Cardwell
Cara Flanagan

Nelson Thorne

a Wolters Kluwer business

Published in 2006 by:
Nelson Thornes Ltd
Delta Place
27 Bath Road
CHELTENHAM
GL53 7TH
United Kingdom

06 07 08 09 10 / 10 9 8 7 6 5 4 3 2 1

A catalogue record for this book is available from the British Library.

ISBN 0 7487 9263 5

Page make-up by GreenGate Publishing Services, Tonbridge, Kent

Printed and bound in Spain by Graphy Cems

Preliminaries

How to use this book	v
The A2 specification	vi
How the exam questions are written	viii
How your examination questions are marked	x
Writing A grade examination essays	xii
Being an effective reviser	xiv
The top eleven tips	xv

Social psychology

Relationships

Attraction and formation

Interpersonal attraction (explanations)	1
Interpersonal attraction (studies)	2
Formation/maintenance (theories)	3

Love and breakdown

Psychological explanations of love	4
The breakdown of relationships (explanations)	5
The breakdown of relationships (studies)	6

Cultural and subcultural differences

The nature of relationships in different cultures (explanations)	7
The nature of relationships in different cultures (studies)	8
Understudied relationships: gay and lesbian relationships	9
Understudied relationships: electronic relationships	10

Pro- and anti-social behaviour

Nature and causes of aggression

Social–psychological theories of aggression	11
Effects of environmental stressors on aggression	12

Altruism and bystander behaviour

Altruism/bystander behaviour (explanations)	13
Altruism/bystander behaviour (studies)	14
Cultural differences in pro-social behaviour	15

Media influences

Pro-social behaviour (explanations)	16
Pro-social behaviour (studies)	17
Anti-social behaviour (explanations)	18
Anti-social behaviour (studies)	19

Physiological psychology

Biological rhythms, sleep and dreams

Biological rhythms

Circadian, infradian and ultradian rhythms	20
Endogenous pacemaker, exogenous zeitgebers	21
Consequences of disrupting rhythms	22

Sleep

Function of sleep: ecological (explanations)	23
Function of sleep: ecological (studies)	24
Function of sleep: restoration (explanations)	25
Function of sleep: restoration (studies)	26

Dreams

The nature of dreams	27
Neurobiological theories of dreaming	28
Psychological theories of dreaming	29

Cognitive psychology

Perceptual processes and development

The visual system

The structure and function of the visual system	30
The nature of visual information processing	31

Perceptual organisation

Theories of visual perception: constructivist theories	32
Theories of visual perception: direct theories	33
Explanations of perceptual organisation	34

Perceptual development

Development of perceptual abilities (studies)	35
Explanations of perceptual development	36
The nature–nurture debate in perception	37

Developmental psychology

Cognitive development

Development of thinking
- Piaget's theory of cognitive development 38
- Vygotsky's theory of cognitive development 39
- Applications of theories of cognitive development 40

Development of intelligence
- The role of genetics in intelligence 41
- Environmental factors in intelligence 42

Development of morality
- Theories of moral understanding/development 43
- Gender and cultural differences 44

Social and personality development

Personality development
- Psychodynamic explanations 45
- Social learning explanations 46

Gender development
- Explanations of gender identity/gender roles 47

Adolescence
- Social development in adolescence 48
- Relationships with parents and peers 49
- Cultural differences in adolescent behaviour 50

Comparative psychology

Evolutionary explanations of human behaviour

Human reproductive behaviour
- Sexual selection and human reproductive behaviour 51
- Evolutionary explanations of parental investment 52

Evolution of mental disorders
- Evolutionary explanations of depression 53
- Evolutionary explanations of anxiety disorders 54

Evolution of intelligence
- Evolutionary factors in human intelligence 55
- Relationship between brain size and intelligence 56

Individual differences

Psychopathology

Schizophrenia, depression, anxiety
- Clinical characteristics 57

Schizophrenia
- Biological explanations of schizophrenia 58
- Psychological explanations of schizophrenia 59

Depression
- Biological explanations of depression 60
- Psychological explanations of depression 61

Anxiety disorders
- Biological explanations of OCD 62
- Psychological explanations of OCD 63

Treating mental disorders

Biological (somatic) therapies
- Chemotherapy 64
- ECT and psychosurgery 65

Behavioural therapies
- Classical conditioning therapies 66
- Operant conditioning therapies 67

Alternative therapies
- Psychodynamic therapies 68
- Cognitive–behavioural therapies 69

Perspectives

Issues and debates

Issues
- Gender bias 70
- Cultural bias 71
- Ethical issues 72
- The use of non-human animals 73

Debates
- Free will and determinism 74
- Reductionism 75
- Psychology as science 76
- Nature–nurture 77

Approaches
- The behavioural approach 78
- The psychodynamic approach 79
- The evolutionary approach 80

This *A2 Mini Companion* covers the most popular subsections of the A2 specification. Each of the subsections (chapters) has been further broken down into divisions following the structure of the specification, and we have further broken down each division into the same topics in the *A2 Complete Companion*.

For each topic we have provided AO1 and AO2 material (on the left and right of each page respectively).

At the bottom of each page there is a range of probable and possible exam questions that could be set. This is not an exhaustive list but gives you the gist of what you may be asked.

There is one other important part of this book. On the next ten pages we outline the 'rules of the game' – the details of the specification, how examination questions are set and marked, and how they should be answered. There are also some thoughts on revision.

Please note that there have been some minor specification changes since the first edition of the *A2 Complete Companion* (see www.aqa.org.uk/qual/gceasa/psyA for the latest version of the AQA A2 specification). We have incorporated these changes into the *A2 Mini Companion* which means there are some small discrepancies between this book and the *A2 Complete Companion*. The changes relate to exams from January 2006 onwards.

Unit 4: 1 exam of 1½ hours
30% of your A2 mark (15% of your overall A level mark)
Answer 3 questions.

Unit 5: 1 exam of 2 hours
40% of your A2 mark (20% of your overall A level mark)
Answer 3 questions.

Unit 6: Coursework
30% of your A2 mark (15% of your overall A level mark)
One piece of coursework, maximum length 2000 words.

The A2 specification, unlike the AS specification, is not entirely compulsory. You are offered some choice about what you can study in the options on Unit 4 and Unit 5.

The specification is divided into:

- Units (e.g. Unit 4)
- Sections (e.g. Social Psychology)
- Subsections (each section is divided into 3 subsections e.g. Relationships)
- Each subsection is further divided into 3; in this book we have called these *divisions*
- We have further separated these divisions into topics (1 per page).

Unit 4 (PYA4)

Unit 4 contains 5 *sections*: Social Psychology, Physiological Psychology, Cognitive Psychology, Developmental Psychology and Comparative Psychology.

Each section is broken down into 3 *subsections*. For example, Social Psychology is divided into: Social cognition, Relationships and Pro- and anti-social behaviour.

You may study all 3 of these subsections from Social Psychology, or alternatively not study any of them at all. There are just 2 requirements regarding the subsections you study for Unit 4:

1 You must study subsections from at least 2 sections of the specification. For example, if you study only 3 subsections they cannot all be from Social Psychology but you could study all 3 of the subsections in Social Psychology plus 1 other subsection. In the exam you would be able to answer only 2 Social Psychology questions and your third question would have to come from another section.

2 You must study a minimum of 3 *subsections*. In the exam you have to answer 3 questions and one question is set on every subsection (5 sections each with three subsections means there are 15 questions on the exam in total). You must ensure that you study every topic in your chosen subsection so that you are able to answer the question set for your subsection. If you study more than three subsections this means you will have a choice in the examination.

There are 5 sections on the Unit 4 exam, and 15 question areas. The minimum requirement is that you study 3 subsections drawn from at least 2 sections. You may, of course, study more than this: for example, 3 subsections in Social Psychology and 1 subsection from another section. If you don't do this you will not be able to answer 3 questions in the examination (and get credit for all 3).

Section A: Social Psychology
1 Social cognition
2 Relationships
3 Pro- and anti-social behaviour

Section B: Physiological Psychology
4 Brain and behaviour
5 Biological rhythms, sleep and dreaming
6 Motivation and emotion

Section C: Cognitive Psychology
7 Attention and pattern recognition
8 Perceptual processes and development
9 Language and thought

Section D: Developmental Psychology
10 Cognitive development
11 Social and personality development
12 Adulthood

Section E: Comparative Psychology
13 Determinants of animal behaviour
14 Animal cognition
15 Evolutionary explanations of human behaviour

N.B. The questions are always numbered on the exam paper in the way indicated here, e.g. the question on the subsection Social and Personality Development is always Question 11.

Unit 5 (PYA5)

This is called the *synoptic paper*. On Unit 5 you have more time to answer each question, the questions are worth more marks and the paper contributes more to your overall A level mark than Unit 4. Your answers are also marked in terms of how *synoptic* they are. You do not need to worry about making your answers *synoptic* because the questions will be set to facilitate such an answer – though it helps to be aware of the fact that you will gain credit for demonstrating your psychology-wide knowledge when answering questions on this paper – relating content to different research methods, issues, debates and/or approaches.

What is synopticity, and why is it important?
Synopticity refers to a broad view of the field of psychology. As this is an advanced level qualification it seems reasonable that, at the end of the course, you should have developed an overview of what psychology is all about. You will learn, over the A level course, about why people forget and about methods of stress management and about explanations of obedience, but what have all these strands of psychology got in common?

These strands of psychology have lots of things in common. All psychologists use similar research methods, they are all concerned with ethical issues in their research, and are also concerned with the different problems that may occur in research (e.g. issues such as gender or cultural bias). Psychologists debate topics such as how (or whether) behaviour is determined and whether nature or nurture offers a better account of behaviour in different areas of psychology. You often encounter the same explanations, such as behaviourist and evolutionary approaches, in different areas of psychology. These are all synoptic topics – the threads that run across the whole specification.

There are three sections on the Unit 5 exam:

Section A: Individual Differences. This is divided into 3 subsections:
1 Issues in the classification and diagnosis of psychological abnormality
2 Psychopathology
3 Treating mental disorders.

In the exam there will be 1 question set for each of these subsections, and you have to answer 1 question. This means you can study just 1 subsection of Individual Differences.

Section B: Issues and Debates. This is divided into 4 issues and 4 debates. In the exam there will be 2 questions on issues (which will be Questions 4 and 5) and 2 questions on debates (which will be Questions 6 and 7).

You have to answer 1 question (either issues or debates). If you study only 3 issues there will be 1 question in the exam that you can answer. The same applies to debates.

Section C: Approaches. This question is different from all the other questions in your exam. You are examined on your ability to apply the basic principles of different approaches in psychology and their related methodologies. You will be given a choice of 2 scenarios (Questions 8 and 9) and asked to answer the following questions:

(a) Describe how the subject presented in the stimulus material might be explained by **two** different approaches. (*6 marks + 6 marks*)

(b) Assess **one** of these explanations of the subject presented in the stimulus material in terms of its strengths and limitations. (*6 marks*)

(c) How might the subject presented in the stimulus material be investigated by one of these approaches? (*6 marks*)

(d) Evaluate the use of this method of investigating the subject presented in the stimulus material. (*6 marks*)

Unit 6 (PYA6)

You must write a report covering a study you have conducted. You may conduct the study with a small group of other students but the report must be individually prepared. Details about designing, conducting, analysing and reporting your coursework are given in *Psychology A2: The Complete Companion*.

1 Injunctions

Injunctions are the command words in exam questions which indicate when you have to provide 'AO1' and 'AO2'. Their meaning is explained in the 'terms used in examination questions' below.

Terms used in examination questions

AO1 terms
Describe, outline, explain, define require you to provide descriptive material.

Note that in addition:

Outline involves a summary description only (more breadth than detail/depth).

Define requires you to state what is meant by a term.

AO2 terms
Evaluate, assess, analyse, to what extent require you to provide AO2 commentary (analysis and/or evaluation).

AO1 and AO2 terms
Discuss, critically consider, compare and contrast require you to provide both AO1 and AO2. Questions may instruct you to discuss with reference to particular criteria, for example, by the use of the phrase '... in terms of ...'.

Note that in addition:

Compare and contrast requires you to demonstrate knowledge and understanding of the stipulated topic areas (AO1) and to consider similarities and/or differences between these (AO2).

An alternative (and equally legitimate) way of answering compare and contrast questions is to demonstrate knowledge and understanding of similarities and differences between the stipulated topic areas (AO1) and to evaluate these similarities and differences (AO2).

2 All questions are set from the specification

If the specification says 'social psychological theories of aggression (e.g. social learning theory)', questions cannot say 'Discuss the social learning theory of aggression' because social learning theory is only given as an *example* in the specification.

If the specification says 'theories of cognitive development, including Piaget' then questions *can* say 'Discuss Piaget's theory of cognitive development' because Piaget's theory is *included* in the specification.

3 AO1 and AO2 are balanced in every question

12 marks for AO1 and AO2 on Unit 4
15 marks for AO1 and AO2 on Unit 5 (except the Approaches question)

Examples:

Critically consider **two or more** explanations of interpersonal attraction.   (24 marks)

In this question there are 12 AO1 marks and 12 AO2 marks – you should describe your explanations and then evaluate them.

(a) Describe **one** study relating to media influences on anti-social behaviour.   (6 marks)

(b) Discuss explanations of media influences on anti-social behaviour.   (18 marks)

In this question there are 12 AO1 marks and 12 AO2 marks; part (a) consists of 6 AO1 marks and part (b) consists of 6 AO1 marks and 12 AO2 marks. (Think: how would this allocation of marks affect the balance of your response?)

(a) Discuss **one** psychological theory of the functions of dreaming.   (12 marks)

(b) Discuss **one** neurobiological theory of the functions of dreaming.   (12 marks)

In this question part (a) consists of 6 AO1 marks and 6 AO2 marks. The same is true of part (b).

4 If a quotation is used in a question there may be a specific instruction for it to be addressed

'Psychology has represented male behaviour as the norm, and consequently has ignored female behaviour and experience.'

Discuss gender bias in **two or more** psychological theories, *with reference to the issues raised* in the quotation above.   (30 marks)

If you are asked a question such as the one above then you will lose AO2 marks if you do not address the quotation (your AO2 marks will be limited to a maximum of 8 out of 12 on PYA4 and 9 out of 15 on PYA5).

However, the question may be:

'Psychology has represented male behaviour as the norm, and consequently has ignored female behaviour and experience.'

Discuss gender bias in **two or more** psychological theories, with *reference to issues such as those raised* in the quotation above.   (30 marks)

In this case there is no requirement to address the quotation. In such cases the quotation is there to provide you with ideas about what you might write.

Always read the *question* first. Never answer the quotation.

5 Numbers are specified where appropriate

It is clearer to ask the question 'Discuss **two** theories of the function of sleep' rather than 'Discuss theories of the function of sleep'. As a result you have clear guidance about the number of theories to include in order to attract the full range of marks.

Sometimes you might be asked 'Discuss **two or more** theories of the function of sleep' in which case you can achieve maximum marks if you cover only two theories but you may also cover more, if you wish.

Your essays are marked using the same assessment objectives as for AS: assessment objective 1 (AO1) and assessment objective 2 (AO2). AO1 is concerned with *description* – assessing your *knowledge and understanding* of psychological principles, perspectives and knowledge. AO2 is concerned with commentary – the *analysis and evaluation* of psychological principles, perspectives and knowledge.

The Unit 4 exam questions are marked out of 24 , with 12 marks for each assessment objective. The Unit 5 exam questions are marked out of 30, with 15 marks for each assessment objective. The mark allocations for both papers are shown below. Although these may look daunting, it is worth remembering that you are likely to achieve a grade A if you perform at the 'slightly limited' level in both AO1 and AO2.

Partial performance
If a question asks for '**two** theories' and you include only 1 theory, you will be marked out of a maximum of 8 marks on AO1 and 8 marks on AO2 (for Unit 5 this is a maximum of 9 for each assessment objective).

This means that when you are asked for 2 theories, the 'first' theory might attract almost two-thirds of the marks. This means that you do not have to present both theories in balance to achieve high marks.

Parted questions
In some cases questions are divided into 2 or more parts. Often part (a) covers the AO1 content of the question (e.g. 'Describe **one** theory of the function of sleep') and part (b) covers the AO2 content (e.g. 'Evaluate the theory of the function of sleep that you described in part (a)'). If you present material in part (a) that is not creditworthy there, but is relevant to part (b), then the examiner will credit the material in the appropriate part. However, you must be careful, because if part (b) was 'Evaluate the theory of the function of sleep in terms of research studies' then the only material that would be creditworthy in part (b) would be evaluation based on research studies. General evaluation, such as in terms of applications, would not be creditworthy in such a question.

Unit 4 (PYA4) Marking allocations

UNIT 4 AO1

Marks	Content	Detail and accuracy	Organisation and structure	Breadth and depth
12–11	Substantial	Accurate and well detailed	Coherent	Substantial evidence of both and balance achieved
10–9	Slightly limited	Accurate and reasonably detailed	Coherent	Evidence of both but imbalanced
8–7	Limited	Generally accurate and reasonably detailed	Reasonably constructed	Increasing evidence of breadth and/or depth
6–5	Basic	Generally accurate, lacks detail	Reasonably constructed	Some evidence of breadth and/or depth
4–3	Rudimentary	Sometimes flawed	Sometimes focused	
2–0	Just discernible	Weak/muddled/inaccurate	Wholly/mainly irrelevant	

UNIT 4 AO2

Marks	Evaluation	Selection and elaboration	Use of material
12–11	Thorough	Appropriate selection and coherent elaboration	Highly effective
10–9	Slightly limited	Appropriate selection and elaboration	Effective
8–7	Limited elaboration	Reasonable	Reasonably effective
6–5	Basic	Some evidence of elaboration	Restricted
4–3	Superficial and rudimentary	No evidence of elaboration	Not effective
2–0	Muddled and incomplete	Wholly or mainly irrelevant	

Unit 5 (PYA5) Marking allocations
UNIT 5 AO1

Marks	Content	Detail and accuracy	Organisation and structure	Breadth/depth of content and synoptic possibilities
15–13	Substantial	Accurate and well detailed	Coherent	Substantial evidence of both
12–10	Slightly limited	Accurate and reasonably detailed	Coherent	Evidence of both
9–7	Limited	Generally accurate and reasonably detailed	Reasonably constructed	Evidence of both
6–4	Basic	Lacking detail	Sometimes focused	Little evidence
3–0	Just discernible	Weak/muddled/inaccurate	Wholly/mainly irrelevant	Little or no evidence

UNIT 5 AO2

Marks	Evaluation	Selection and elaboration	Use of material and synoptic possibilities
15–13	Thorough	Appropriate selection and coherent elaboration	Highly effective
12–10	Slightly limited	Appropriate selection and elaboration	Effective
9–7	Limited elaboration	Reasonably effective	Reasonably
6–4	Basic	Some evidence of elaboration	Restricted
3–0	Weak, muddled and incomplete	Wholly or mainly irrelevant	Not effective

Unit 5 (PYA5) The approaches question
Part (a)

Marks	Content	Accuracy	Engagement
6–5	Reasonably thorough	Accurate	Coherent
4–3	Limited	Generally accurate	Reasonable
2–1	Basic	Sometimes flawed/inaccurate	Muddled
0			No engagement

Part (b) and Part (d)

Marks	Commentary	Use of material	Engagement
6–5	Reasonably thorough	Effective	Coherent
4–3	Limited	Reasonably effective	Reasonable
2–1	Basic	Restricted	Muddled
0			No engagement

Part (c)

Marks	Commentary	Plausibility	Engagement
6–5	Reasonably thorough	Appropriate	Coherent
4–3	Limited	Reasonably appropriate	Reasonable
2–1	Basic	Largely inappropriate	Muddled
0			No engagement

How to produce good AO1 material
Try to provide depth and breadth

If you are asked to 'Discuss research studies related to social–psychological theories of aggression' then you might describe and evaluate 10 different studies but, in the 15 minutes allocated to AO1 on Unit 4, you would have little time to do more than give the briefest description of these studies. In other words, you would provide lots of *breadth* and little *depth* (detail). It is better to cover fewer studies and therefore more details of each study. The examiners know how much time you have; they accept that there must be a trade-off between breadth and depth. The best essays provide evidence of both.

Structure your essay

AO1 is not just about knowledge and understanding, it is also about how well structured your answer is (i.e. how logically you unfold your material in response to the question). Structure is a way to demonstrate a good grasp of a topic (your knowledge and understanding), so it is reasonable to judge AO1 quality in terms of structure as well as depth and breadth of information.

How to produce effective AO2 material
Effective use of material

You might be asked a part (b) AO2 question 'To what extent do research studies support the view that the media are responsible for anti-social behaviour?'. In this case you are required to select appropriate research studies and *use this material* (not describe it) to present an argument that shows that the media is (or is not) responsible for anti-social behaviour. If you only *describe* research studies your answer will receive a maximum of 4 marks out of 12 from AO2 (6 marks out of 15 on Unit 5).

The AO2 description trap

There are other situations where candidates feel drawn into *describing* AO2 material rather than using it as part of a sustained critical commentary. For example, you may be answering a question 'Discuss Piaget's theory of cognitive development' and wish to evaluate this by saying 'On the other hand there are other theories of cognitive development such as Vygotsky's. Vygotsky proposed that mental abilities …' A candidate who simply *describes* alternative theories (or appropriate research evidence) will receive very few marks for AO2.

Coherent elaboration

Coherent elaboration is another of the criteria used to mark AO2. There is very limited credit for presenting comments such as 'One limitation of this study was that it lacked ecological validity' or 'One strength of this theory is that it can be applied to the real world'. To attract higher marks you must offer some *elaboration*. In the examples above the candidate has merely *identified* the criticism. What we now need to see is a justification of the criticism and an explanation of why this is a limitation or strength (see the illustration in box below).

Three-point rule for elaborating criticisms

Identify the criticism: 'One limitation of this study was that it lacked ecological validity'
Justify the criticism: 'because other studies conducted in different settings have generally failed to produce the same results'
Explain the criticism: 'which means you cannot generalise the findings to other settings'

Identify the criticism: 'One strength of this theory is that it can be applied to the real world'
Justify the criticism: 'such as in teaching where it has led to child-centred education'
Explain the criticism: 'as a result it revolutionised primary school teaching'.

There is no difference between AO1 and AO2 material

The difference lies in the way you use the material. For example, if you describe a research study, you are likely to be given AO1 credit, but if you use a research study as commentary on an AO1 point then it will be given AO2 credit, for example:

All AO1 credit:

'Social learning theory proposes that we acquire new behaviours through observation and indirect reinforcement. Bandura conducted a study where children became more aggressive when they saw someone else behave aggressively towards a Bobo doll.'

A mixture of AO1 and AO2 because the study has been used differently:

'Social learning theory proposes that we acquire new behaviours through observation and indirect reinforcement. This was demonstrated in a study by Bandura where children became more aggressive when they saw someone else behave aggressively towards a Bobo doll.'

In this book we have made a point of presenting all AO2 material in an effective manner by using the all-important 'lead-in' phrases shown in the AO2 exercise on the right.

How to put this together in the exam

There is no doubt that planning helps. In an exam you should:
1 Look at the question and underline the key words. For example 'Describe and evaluate **two** explanations of the function of sleep'.
2 Decide on a structure for your answer. This may vary in relation to the question that was asked, as illustrated in the possible essay plans below. Every answer plan below is based on the notion that 600 words is about right for a 30-minute answer [Unit 4].

AO2 exercise

'Discuss research studies relating to media influence on anti-social behaviour.'

Answer: *Many studies have been carried out into the effects of the media. One such study was conducted by Parke et al. in 1977. This looked at a group of delinquent male adolescents living in an institution. A measure was taken of their aggression levels before the study started. One group was shown violent videos and the other group were shown non-violent videos. The researchers found that aggression increased in the first group.*

What AO2 statements could you provide? Below are a list of useful phrases to 'kick-start' AO2. Try using some of them to provide appropriate commentary.

'This suggests that …'

'Therefore we can conclude …'

'This supports the theory that …'

'There were flaws in the methodology, e.g. …'

'An important ethical consideration is …'

'Further support comes from …'

'Another psychologist disagreed, arguing that …'

'This has important applications in …'

'One consequence of this is …'

'The advantage of this study is …'

'One limitation of this study is …'

'An alternative explanation could be …'

'Not everyone reacts the same way …'

'This has been applied to …'

'There may be cultural variations …'

'The study lacked ecological validity because …'

Discuss one theory of …

AO1: 3 paragraphs of 100 words each, or 6 paragraphs. In each paragraph identify a feature of the theory.

AO2: 3 paragraphs of 100 words each, identifying and explaining three criticisms.

Discuss one theory of …

AO1: 6 paragraphs of 50 words each. In each paragraph identify a feature of the theory.

AO2: After each AO1 point write 50 words of commentary.

Discuss two theories of …

Theory 1:
AO1: 3 paragraphs of 50 words each.
AO2: 3 paragraphs of 50 words.

Theory 2:
AO1: 3 paragraphs of 50 words each.
AO2: 3 paragraphs of 50 words.

Discuss two theories of …

Theory 1:
AO1: 4 paragraphs of 50 words each.
AO2: 4 paragraphs of 50 words.

Theory 2:
AO1: 2 paragraphs of 50 words each.
AO2: 2 paragraphs of 50 words.

When revising for your A2 psychology exam, don't engage in random activities, but be systematic in your use of time. The table below shows how you might divide up 18 hours of revision (perhaps over 3 or 4 days) on Pro- and anti-social behaviour (Chapter 2). Note how specific time slots are allocated for specific topics and skills.

- *Revise actively:* It is important to process information.
- *Read lots of accounts:* Each account is different and helps you to process the information and get new ideas that are more meaningful to you.
- *Be 'multi-sensory':* Work with the senses best for you – visual diagrams, word lists or even auditory cues (say it out loud).
- *Work for realistic intervals:* Don't kid yourself that three hours spent in front of your books equals three hours of revision.
- *Don't gamble on topics:* Questions are not set to a pattern. Never leave any topic out because it came up last time.
- *Revision is a skill:* Treat revision as a skill like any other.
- *Practise with others:* Discussing essays and notes with others helps you process material.

	A day in the life of ... 'Pro- and anti-social behaviour'	
	9 × 2 hours	*18 × 1 hour*
Nature and causes of aggression	Social psychological theories of aggression	Knowledge and understanding (AO1) Analysis and evaluation (AO2)
	Research into the effects of environmental stressors on aggressive behaviour	Knowledge and understanding (AO1) Analysis and evaluation (AO2)
Altruism and bystander behaviour	Explanations relating to human altruism/bystander behaviour	Knowledge and understanding (AO1) Analysis and evaluation (AO2)
	Research studies relating to human altruism/bystander behaviour	Knowledge and understanding (AO1) Analysis and evaluation (AO2)
	Cultural differences in pro-social behaviour	Knowledge and understanding (AO1) Analysis and evaluation (AO2)
Media influences on pro- and anti-social behaviour	Explanations relating to media influences on pro-social behaviour	Knowledge and understanding (AO1) Analysis and evaluation (AO2)
	Research studies relating to media influences on pro-social behaviour	Knowledge and understanding (AO1) Analysis and evaluation (AO2)
	Explanations relating to media influences on anti-social behaviour	Knowledge and understanding (AO1) Analysis and evaluation (AO2)
	Research studies relating to media influences on anti-social behaviour	Knowledge and understanding (AO1) Analysis and evaluation (AO2)

1 Learn the material. There is no substitute for knowing the facts. However, a clever student finds ways to gain this knowledge effortlessly. Use the 'levels of processing approach' – the more you process the information in a meaningful way, the more it will be engraved in your memory without having to sit for hours trying to force the knowledge in.

2 Process things 'meaningfully'. Do revision tasks that mean you have to think, such as writing lists of key words, writing MCQ questions, delivering a short talk to a group. Organisation, elaboration and effort all lead to deep processing. Rote-learned material is quickly forgotten when people feel anxious – like in an exam.

3 In the exam choose your questions carefully. You may not have any choice about which questions to answer, but if you do it is worth spending time fully considering what material you know for each question.

4 Manage time effectively in the exam. In the examination you must write neither more nor less than is indicated by the marks for the question. You have 30 minutes for each question on Unit 4. This includes *thinking* and *planning* as well as writing time. For Unit 5 questions you have 40 minutes.

5 Read the question carefully. How many times have you been told this? But it is true. Candidates see a question with the word '... ethical issues ...' and write all they know about ethical issues – but what if the question was about ethical issues in psychological studies? You must *shape* your knowledge to fit the question asked – not answer the question you would have liked to be asked.

6 The three-point rule. A key criterion for AO2 is elaboration. Candidates frequently lose marks because they don't elaborate their commentary. You should always (1) name your criticism (positive or negative), (2) justify your criticism – provide evidence to support your claim of why it is a weakness/strength in this theory/study, and (3) explain your criticism – why is it a good or bad thing? So if your criticism of a study is 'lack of ecological validity' then you have named it. You need to demonstrate in what way it does occur in this study ('The study involved rating people in a laboratory setting which doesn't reflect how relationships are really formed'). Finally you need to indicate why lack of ecological validity is a bad thing ('Low ecological validity means that we cannot generalise these findings to real life').

7 Produce effective AO2. There is actually nothing set in stone as 'AO2': it is all about how you use it. For example, a study could be *described* as part of the AO1 content of your answer or could be used as *commentary* depending on how you introduce the material into your essay. Use AO2 phrases such as 'however' or 'this is supported by' in order to turn AO1 material into AO2. You should also avoid describing AO2 studies/theories: this is not appropriate for AO2 points.

8 Breadth and depth. In the same way that elaboration is important for good AO2 marks, detail is important for AO1 marks. 'Detail' doesn't mean writing lots and lots. It means using precise psychological terms and different aspects of a theory or study. It is a mistake to write about lots of studies – it is better to write about fewer studies but provide more details for each study. But you shouldn't spend a whole essay writing about one study. You have to get the balance right.

9 The three bears rule. Never write too much or too little. Get it just right: enough detail for all the marks available but not more than this (even if you would like to impress the examiner with all you know). And don't include material that is not relevant.

10 Manage stress effectively. You have studied stress management (or you should have at AS) so apply this knowledge. A moderate level of stress/anxiety is good for performance. An athlete running a race depends on adrenaline to enhance performance. Adrenaline in moderate levels is also good for thinking but too much stress depresses performance. Write your own list of ways that you might reduce stress in the exam.

11 Motivate yourself. People do well when they are highly motivated. Find *some* reason for why you really really want to succeed. It also helps to think positively and believe in your own ability. High achievers have high self-esteem.

Chapter 1	Attraction and formation >	Interpersonal attraction (explanations)
Social psychology	Love and breakdown	Interpersonal attraction (studies)
Relationships >	Cultural and subcultural differences	Formation/maintenance (theories)

Explanation 1: Personal characteristics

In a nutshell – We are attracted to people who possess particular types of personal characteristics.

Physical attractiveness
People who are attractive possess characteristics that promote breeding success (evolutionary significance).

The halo effect
If people are physically attractive, we attribute other positive characteristics to them, and so are more likely to be attracted to them.

The matching hypothesis
We are attracted to those who closely match our perceptions of our own level of physical attractiveness.

Personality
There are cultural differences in what constitutes an 'attractive' personality. Extroversion is valued in Western cultures.

Attractiveness is important because ... people who are physically attractive gain other advantages, although research also suggests that attractive people may be seen as egoistic by others.

It appears to be universal because ... there is evidence that certain similar traits are rated as attractive in different cultures (Langlois and Roggmann, 1990).

Supported by ... Wheeler and Kim (1997), who found that physically attractive individuals are seen as possessing traits viewed positively in that culture.

Supported by ... Walster et al. (1966), who found that at a 'computer dance', physical attractiveness was more important than matching. If participants were given choice and met beforehand, matching was more apparent (Walster and Walster, 1969).

However ... Felmlee (1995) found that some initially attractive personality characteristics may become less attractive over time and this may lead to dissolution.

Explanation 2: Evolutionary explanations

In a nutshell – Adaptive mechanisms that evolved in the EEA (environment of evolutionary adaption) are still seen as guiding mate choice today.

Evolutionarily significant characteristics
Men should seek signs of reproductive value (age and healthiness). Women should be attracted to males who have characteristics that indicate social and economic advantages. Mechanisms that evolved in the EEA are still seen as guiding mate choice today.

Parental investment
As males invest less (biologically) than females, males should be concerned with *quantity* of mates, and females *quality* of mates.

A consequence is that ... men become more concerned with sexual infidelity in their partner (risk of cuckoldry), women with emotional infidelity (possible loss of resources) (Buss et al., 1992).

Supported by ... research evidence from personal ads (Waynforth and Dunbar, 1995) which shows that women advertise their attractiveness (signifying fertility) whereas men advertise their economic status (signifying resources).

Alternative explanation of interpersonal attraction
Research suggests that sexual attraction may also be influenced by the action of *pheromones* rather than personal characteristics or evolutionarily significant factors alone.

Probable questions
1. Describe and evaluate **one or more** explanations of interpersonal attraction. (24 marks)
2. Discuss psychological research (explanations **and/or** studies) into interpersonal attraction. (24 marks)

Possible questions
3. Outline and evaluate **two** explanations of interpersonal attraction. (24 marks)

1

Chapter 1	Attraction and formation >	Interpersonal attraction (explanations)
Social psychology	Love and breakdown	**Interpersonal attraction (studies)**
Relationships >	Cultural and subcultural differences	Formation/maintenance (theories)

Studies 1: Proximity

Being in physical proximity to another person is a powerful determinant of attraction.

Liking

Festinger et al. (1950) – students who lived at the foot of the stairs had more friends than others on the same floor. Segal (1974) – physical proximity had stronger effect on attraction than any other characteristic.

Disliking

Ebbesen et al. (1976) found that not only the most liked others lived close by, but also the most disliked others.

> *Explained by … filter theory*
> Proximity may act as an initial filter for relationships, and may act as both a positive and negative factor in their development.

> *Is the proximity effect due to similarity or familiarity?*
> As similar people congregate together, proximity effects may simply be similarity effects. However, Byrne (1961) found proximity to be more influential.

> *This can be explained more by …* people living close to us having a greater potential for engaging in behaviours that annoy us; therefore physical proximity may also increase the likelihood of *disliking* someone else.

Studies 2: Familiarity

- The *mere exposure* explanation was tested in a study of student residences in an Israeli university (Yinon et al., 1977): the higher the level of interaction allowed by living arrangements, the more likely that students would form friendships with others within the same residential unit.

- Mita et al. (1977) found that participants preferred a mirror-image photograph of themselves (more familiar because they saw themselves in a mirror), while their friends liked the normal photograph for the same reason.

> *However …* Swap (1977) found that repeated exposure to someone who punished a participant resulted in greater *disliking*.

> *Importance of familiarity*
> - Familiarity leads to predictability, which eliminates guesswork and risk.
> - During exposure to a person we may become directly or indirectly conditioned (reinforcement-affect).

Studies 3: Similarity

Similarity of attitudes is an important ingredient in initial attraction and the formation of relationships.

Similarity and attraction

Similarity of attitudes and background is important in *initial* attraction (Newcomb, 1961) and in long-term relationships (Kerckhoff, 1974).

Dissimilarity and repulsion

Research (e.g. Singh and Tan, 1992) has shown that whereas *similarity* of attitudes leads to greater attraction, discovery of a higher proportion of *dissimilarities* leads to less attraction (i.e. repulsion).

> *Importance of similarity*
> - Being with similar people makes us feel our own characteristics are acceptable.
> - We may avoid dissimilar things because discrepancy is uncomfortable.

> *However …* research does not always support the repulsion hypothesis. Smeaton et al. (1989) found that only similarity was important in liking (dissimilarity was ignored).

Studies 4: Suitability

Cameron et al. (1977) found that men stressed status in lonely heart ads, whereas women tended to emphasise their physical appearance.
Duck (1999), in an overview of research in this area, found that personal advertisers conformed to current cultural beliefs about suitable partners.

> *Biology or culture?*
> - Cross-cultural research (Buss, 1989) suggests that male and female preferences are the same all over the world.
> - However, there are significant cultural and historical trends in what counts as attractive and therefore suitable.

Probable questions

1. Describe and evaluate research studies into interpersonal attraction. *(24 marks)*
2. (a) Outline **two** explanations of interpersonal attraction. *(12 marks)*

   (b) Evaluate the **two** explanations of interpersonal attraction that you outlined in (a) in terms of relevant research studies. *(12 marks)*

Possible questions

3. (a) Outline and evaluate **one or more** explanations of interpersonal attraction. *(12 marks)*

   (b) Outline and evaluate research studies relating to interpersonal attraction. *(12 marks)*

Chapter 1 | Attraction and formation > | Interpersonal attraction (explanations)
Social psychology | Love and breakdown | Interpersonal attraction (studies)
Relationships > | Cultural and subcultural differences | Formation/maintenance (theories)

Theory 1: Reinforcement affect model (Byrne and Clore, 1970)

In a nutshell – We enter into a relationship because the individual concerned creates positive feelings in us, which makes them more attractive to us.

1. **Operant conditioning** We like some individuals because they provide us with direct reinforcement (i.e. they make us feel good).
2. **Classical conditioning** We like some individuals because they are associated with pleasant events.
3. **Affect** These feelings lead to either a positive (if they make us feel happy) or negative (if they make us feel unhappy) evaluation of the individual concerned.

Limitations
- Explores only one factor that may affect liking.
- Probably only relevant to certain kinds of relationship.
- Does not account for gender and cultural differences.

This is supported by ... Griffit and Guay (1969) who found that participants rated an experimenter more highly if he/she had given them a positive evaluation.

This is supported by ... Griffit and Guay (1969) who found that onlookers were also rated more highly when the experimenter had rated participants positively.

This is supported by ... Cunningham (1988), who found that men who watched a happy movie later interacted more positively with a female and disclosed more to her.

Commentary on learning theory
Learning theory, which underlies this approach, is supported by well-controlled experimental research.

Theory 2: Social exchange theory (Thibault and Kelley, 1959)

In a nutshell – The formation of relationships is a two-way process, involving an interaction between two partners, each with their own needs and expectations.

Stages in the development of a relationship
Thibault and Kelley (1959) believed there were four stages in the development of a relationship – sampling, bargaining, commitment and institutionalisation.

Profit and loss
In any relationship, individuals try to maximise their rewards (profit) and minimise their costs (loss).

Comparison level (CL)
A product of our experiences in other relationships together with what we might expect from this one. Relationships that exceed our CL are judged worthwhile.

Strengths
- This theory is relevant to many different kinds of relationship.
- It can explain individual differences between and within individuals.

Limitations
- The theory ignores the social aspects of a relationship.
- It focuses only on the selfish nature of relationships.
- It ignores 'fairness of exchange' rather than simply seeking a profit.

This is supported by ... Rusbult and Martz (1995) who used this theory to explain why some women stay in abusive relationships.

However ... Aronson and Linder (1965) found that increases in reward, rather than constant reward, are crucial.

This is supported by ... Simpson et al. (1990) found participants who were involved in a relationship gave lower attractiveness ratings of possible opposite sex alternatives (presumably to protect their own relationships).

Probable questions
1. Outline and evaluate **two** theories of the formation **and/or** maintenance of relationships. (24 marks)
2. Outline and evaluate **two** or more theories of the formation **and/or** maintenance of relationships. (24 marks)

Possible questions
3. Describe and evaluate **one** theory of the formation **and/or** maintenance of relationships. (24 marks)

Chapter 1	Attraction and formation	**Psychological explanations of love**
Social psychology	**Love and breakdown** >	The breakdown of relationships (explanations)
Relationships >	Cultural and subcultural differences	The breakdown of relationships (studies)

Explanation 1: The triangular theory of love (STERNBERG 1986)

In a nutshell – Love consists of three components, the combination of which determines the *type* of love.

Three components of love
- **Intimacy** a feeling of closeness between partners
- **Passion** the drive that leads to romantic and physical attraction
- **Commitment** – making a decision to stay with partner

Typology of love relationships
Consummate (complete) love involves all three components. If one or more is absent, a different type of love exists.
Successful relationships tend to be those where a person's current relationship matches their 'ideal' relationship.

Love as a story
Sternberg also believed that people learn about love from books, parents and from television. This gives them romantic expectations of what love *should* be like.

Cultural differences
Passion is most important at the outset of Western relationships, whereas in non-Western relationships, commitment is most important.

Research support
Although Sternberg based this typology on students and adults in the Yale University community, other research (Fehr, 1988) has supported his findings.

However ... although happy couples appear to endorse similar *kinds* of story, there are gender differences in what men and women believe to be important in love.

An alternative explanation
Alternative theories have tended to be simpler. Three factor theory sees love as a label we place on physiological arousal in situations that cultural learning tells us may be love (Hatfield and Walster, 1981).

Explanation 2: Love as an attachment process (HAZAN AND SHAVER, 1987)

In a nutshell – Love is seen as an extension of early attachment styles.

Early attachment styles (Ainsworth, 1967)
From observations of babies and their mothers, Ainsworth produced three distinct attachment styles – *secure, insecure–resistant* and *insecure–avoidant*.

Love as attachment – the continuity hypothesis
Later relationships are likely to be characterised by a continuation of early attachment styles as the mother's behaviour creates an *internal working model* of relationships for the child.

Different aspects of love (Shaver et al., 1988)
What we experience as 'love' is an integration of three learned behavioural systems – *attachment, caregiving* and *sexuality*.
These three aspects influence the development of different subtypes of love.

Research support for continuity hypothesis
Hazan and Shaver (1987) found that adults who had been securely attached were more successful in adult relationships than those who had been insecurely attached. These findings have been supported in other studies (e.g. Feeney and Noller, 1990).

Limitations of continuity hypothesis
- Most studies (such as Hazan and Shaver) rely on *retrospective* classification – which may be flawed due to faulty recollections. However, *longitudinal* studies (e.g. McCarthy, 1999) support the main claims of this hypothesis.
- Such research is only correlational, so we cannot claim a cause–effect relationship.

Probable questions
1. Outline and evaluate **two or more** psychological explanations of love. *(24 marks)*
2. Describe and evaluate **one or more** psychological explanations of love. *(24 marks)*

Possible questions
3. 'Psychologists have struggled to understand that most human of emotions – love'.
   Critically consider psychological research (explanations and/or studies) into the nature of love. *(24 marks)*

4

napter 1 | Attraction and formation | Psychological explanations of love
ocial psychology | Love and breakdown > | **The breakdown of relationships (explanations)**
elationships > | Cultural and subcultural differences | The breakdown of relationships (studies)

Explanation 1: Reasons for relationship breakdown (DUCK, 1999)

In a nutshell – Research has established a number of reasons why relationships typically break down.

Lack of skills
Relationships are difficult for some people because they lack the interpersonal skills (e.g. they are poor conversationalists) to make them mutually satisfying.

Lack of stimulation
People expect relationships to change and develop, and their not doing so is seen as sufficient justification to end the relationship.

Maintenance difficulties
In some circumstances (e.g. long-distance relationships), people cannot give their relationship the constant maintenance that it needs.

Cultural differences
These factors may only apply to Western cultures. In non-Western cultures, other factors (e.g. family and community pressure) are involved.

Gender differences
Women tend to stress unhappiness and incompatibility as reasons for dissolution whereas men are upset by 'sexual withholding' (Brehm and Kassin, 1996).

However ... fatal attraction theory (Felmlee, 1995) predicts that the factors that initially led to attraction (e.g. lively behaviour) will become the ones that cause dissolution.

However ... research suggests that long-distance relationships are not doomed because people use many different maintenance strategies to preserve them (Holt and Stone, 1988).

Explanation 2: Stage model of dissolution (DUCK, 1999)

In a nutshell
- Partners frequently feel uneasy about a relationship before dissolution begins.
- All relationships exist within a social matrix.
- People are motivated to justify their own actions in this process.

Intrapsychic phase
The person begins to reflect on the deficiencies of his or her relationship, but does not yet face his or her partner about these.

Dyadic phase
The person confronts his/her partner. The relationship can still be repaired at this stage.

Social phase
Dissatisfaction spills over to family and friends who may take sides.

Grave-dressing phase
Each partner strives to construct his/her *own* version of the failed relationship.

Strengths
- This model emphasises that relationship dissolution is not sudden but *a process*.
- It identifies places where things start to go wrong – and can be applied to relationship counselling.

Limitations
Duck's stage model does not explain *why* relationships break down (see Duck's *reasons for relationship breakdown* above), nor does it tend to be supported by research evidence.

An alternative model: Lee (1984)
- Lee's model places more emphasis on the early stages of breakdown when there is still hope that the relationship might be saved.
- Contrary to Duck's predictions, Lee found that many people go directly from dissatisfaction to termination without going through any intermediate stages.

Probable questions
1. Outline and evaluate **two or more** explanations relating to the breakdown of relationships. (24 marks)
2. (a) Outline **one or more** theories relating to the breakdown of relationships. (12 marks)
   (b) Evaluate the **one or more** theories of the breakdown of relationships that you outlined in (a) in terms of relevant research studies. (12 marks)

Possible questions
3. (a) Outline and evaluate **one or more** explanations relating to the breakdown of relationships. (12 marks)
   (b) Outline and evaluate research studies relating to the breakdown of relationships. (12 marks)

Chapter 1
Social psychology
Relationships >

Attraction and formation
Love and breakdown >
Cultural and subcultural differences

Psychological explanations of love
The breakdown of relationships (explanations)
The breakdown of relationships (studies)

Study 1: Rule violation
Argyle and Henderson (1984) found that critical rule violations included jealousy and lack of tolerance for a relationship with a third party.

However ... this study also found important *individual differences* including age and gender differences.

Study 2: Letting go and moving on
As people enter new situations they encounter others that are more rewarding than their current relationship (Hays and Oxley, 1986).

This suggests that ... dissolution is seen as a necessary and potentially *growth-enhancing* aspect of an individual's development.

Study 3: Long-distance relationships
Shaver et al. (1985) surveyed 400 first-year students at the University of Denver and found that half of these students attributed the break-up of a romantic relationship to their move away to university.

This might be explained by ... the fact that the opportunity to be in new relationships is too distracting as is the pressure to develop relationships that are more convenient to maintain.

Study 4: Evidence relating to Duck's model
Masuda (2001) tested the validity of Duck's model in Japan, and found that it applied equally well in Japanese as it does in Western cultures.

However ... there are differences. In Japan, as in other collectivist cultures, the social network plays a more prominent part in helping the couple work through problems before they get out of hand.

Study 5: Sequences of separation (LEE, 1984)
- Dissatisfaction (D)
- Exposure (E)
- Negotiation (N)
- Resolution (R)
- Termination (T)

E and N were found to be the most intense stages.

However ... despite very detailed data obtained in this study, couples were not married and therefore constitute a *biased sample*.

Contrary to predictions in Duck's model ... Lee found that many people go directly from dissatisfaction (D) to termination (T) without going through any intermediate stages.

Study 6: A mathematical model of relationship breakdown
Gottman et al. (2004) found that the way partners responded to each other enabled them to develop an equation whereby they could predict the likelihood of future breakdown.

The model is useful because ... it could be used to show couples seeking counselling how they might get on better.

However ... the researchers admit that the model might not work well in cultural contexts outside the US.

Study 7: Lack of skills
Leary et al. (1986) found that bores tend to put other people off because of their egocentrism and inability to put themselves into another person's shoes.

This might be explained by ... when people appear to be uninterested in us, we are more likely to be uninterested in them and are less likely to continue a relationship with them.

Study 8: Grave-dressing
La Gaipa (1982) found that a necessary part of leaving a relationship is *face-saving*, the need for each person to exit a relationship with his/her reputation of relationship reliability intact.

However ... although the primary role of this process is face-saving, it also serves to keep certain memories alive and to justify the commitment to the original partner.

Probable questions
1. Describe and evaluate research studies relating to the breakdown of relationships. *(24 marks)*

Possible questions
2. (a) Outline and evaluate **one or more** explanations relating to the breakdown of relationships. *(12 marks)*

   (b) Outline and evaluate research studies relating to the breakdown of relationships. *(12 marks)*

Chapter 1 | Attraction and formation | **Relationships in different cultures (explanations)**
Social psychology | Love and breakdown | Relationships in different cultures (studies)
Relationships > | Cultural and subcultural differences > | Understudied relationships (gay and lesbian)
| | Understudied relationships (electronic)

In a nutshell – Given that Western and non-Western cultures differ in so many ways, we might expect to find differences in the way relationships are viewed and acted out.

Explanation 1: Voluntary or non-voluntary

Western cultures appear to be characterised by a higher degree of choice in personal relationships and a greater 'pool' of potential relationships than in non-Western cultures, where relationships are determined by other factors.

However ... many 'involuntary' non-Western relationships still appear to be successful and partners report 'falling in love' (Epstein, 2002).

This distinction is an over-simplification ... because of the similarity of the partners (background, education, religion, etc.). Many Western relationships are actually 'semi-arranged'.

Explanation 2: Individual or group-based

Western cultures place greater importance on individual satisfaction in relationships, whereas non-Western cultures place greater emphasis on the satisfaction of more collective (i.e. group-based) goals.

Despite this distinction ... many collectivist cultures are becoming more individualist and therefore relationships are becoming less group-based, as is evident in changing trends in Israeli kibbutzim (Adar, 2002).

Explanation 3: Continuity and discontinuity

Non-Western cultures, which emphasise continuity, are likely to be dominated by *permanent* relationships. Western cultures, which emphasise change and discontinuity, are likely to favour *temporary* relationships.

However ... the discontinuity evident in non-Western relationships is a relatively recent phenomenon, indicating that this may be due more to changes in urbanisation than to cultural differences between Western and non-Western cultures.

Explanation 4: Attitudes to romantic love

Romantic love does not appear to be an essential ingredient of relationships in collectivist cultures, but as these societies become more urbanised (and therefore more individualistic), romantic love becomes more important.

The importance of romantic love can be explained by ... the spread of urbanisation (i.e. choice) and media influences, both of which are increasing in non-Western cultures.

However ... the validity of cross-cultural research on relationships is limited because participants may have quite different social backgrounds.

Explanation 5: Different styles of marriage

Although monogamy is the dominant style of marriage in the West, polygyny (one man, more than one wife) is more common in some other cultures.

A consequence of cultural differences is that ... individualism creates barriers to healthy relationships because of each partner's need for autonomy. This may push up divorce rates (Dion and Dion, 1988) in the West.

Probable questions

1. Describe and evaluate research (explanations **and/or** studies) relating to the nature of relationships in different cultures. *(24 marks)*

2. (a) Outline **two** explanations relating to the formation of relationships. *(12 marks)*

   (b) To what extent have research studies demonstrated variations in the nature of relationships in different cultures? *(12 marks)*

Possible questions

3. Outline and evaluate **two or more** explanations of the nature of relationships in different cultures. *(24 marks)*

4. Critically consider research studies relating to the nature of relationships in different cultures. *(24 marks)*

Chapter 1
Social psychology
Relationships >

Attraction and formation
Love and breakdown
Cultural and subcultural differences >

Relationships in different cultures (explanations)
Relationships in different cultures (studies)
Understudied relationships (gay and lesbian)
Understudied relationships (electronic)

In a nutshell – Researchers have established differences in the norms and rules of relationships across cultures, but cross-cultural studies are also prone to methodological problems.

Study 1: Cultural norms
The *norm of reciprocity* appears to be almost universal, but there are cultural differences. In individualist cultures, voluntary reciprocity is the norm, whereas in collectivist cultures reciprocity in personal relationships is more obligatory (Ting-Toomey, 1986).

Supported by ... Argyle (1982), who found evidence of formal norms concerning the giving of gifts and for reciprocating in Japanese but not Western cultures.

However ... Takano and Osaka (1999) reviewed 15 studies that compared the US and Japan, and found little evidence of an individualist/collectivist distinction in these cultures.

Study 2: Rules
• Rules define the responsibilities of each partner in a relationship.
• Argyle *et al.* (1986) found differences in relationship rules across different cultures, but also many similarities (e.g. showing courtesy and respect and avoiding social intimacy).

These findings are consistent with ... differences predicted from the individualism/collectivism distinction.

However ... psychological research may have exaggerated the differences between Western and non-Western cultures in that research has focused on the experiences of students, who represent a biased sample.

Study 3: Subcultural differences in friendships
• Friendship appears more important to the middle class, while kin is to the working class. Shucksmith *et al.* (1993) found that young people from middle-class backgrounds spent longer in mixed-sex groups.
• Middle-class friends selected on the basis of shared interests and attitudes; working-class friendships were more based on location.

This may be due to the fact that ... children from middle-class backgrounds are more likely to go to university and so anticipate a longer period before they settle down.

However ... there are gender differences in the nature of friendships, with boys placing more value on looking and behaving like their friends and girls more on the personality of their friends (Shucksmith *et al.*, 1993).

Study 4: Subcultural differences in marital relationships
Shucksmith *et al.* (1993) found that middle-class marriages are more symmetrical than working-class marriages, with husbands and wives sharing friends, leisure activities and making joint decisions.

However ... Piatt (2005) claims that we know little about how husbands and wives experience their roles in different ethnic groups, which limits the extent to which this finding applies to other groups.

Study 5: Subcultural differences in relationships with children
Shucksmith *et al.* (1993) found that middle-class families tend to be more child-centred with fathers playing a more significant role than in working-class families.

This might be explained by ... the discovery that the more traditional the sex-role ideology of the household, the less involved the father is in childcare (Davis and Perkins, 1996).

Probable questions
1. Critically consider research studies relating to the nature of relationships in different cultures. *(24 marks)*
2. (a) Outline **two** explanations relating to the formation of relationships. *(12 marks)*
   (b) To what extent have research studies demonstrated variations in the nature of relationships in different cultures? *(12 marks)*

Possible questions
3. (a) Outline and evaluate **one or more** explanations relating to the nature of relationships in different cultures. *(12 marks)*
   (b) Outline and evaluate **one or more** studies relating to the nature of relationships in different cultures. *(12 marks)*

Chapter 1
Social psychology
Relationships   >

Attraction and formation
Love and breakdown
Cultural and subcultural differences >

Relationships in different cultures (explanations)
Relationships in different cultures (studies)
Understudied relationships (gay and lesbian)
Understudied relationships (electronic)

Formation

Dating patterns
- The gay subculture is associated with a liberal attitude to casual sex, but gay men have shown an increasing tendency toward *emotional* rather than sexual intimacy.

- In common with many women, lesbians have been socialised into *reactive* rather than *proactive* dating behaviour (Kitzinger and Coyle, 1995).

Preference for partners
- Gay men appear to desire specific *physical* attributes in a potential partner (Davidson 1991).

- Lesbians are more likely to emphasise *personality* characteristics than physical appearance (Huston and Schwartz, 1995).

A consequence of this is ... that establishing long-term relationships becomes particularly difficult for adolescent homosexuals, who must first make the decision to 'come out', and then attempt to meet other homosexuals.

This finding is consistent with evolutionary theory ... since male and female homosexuals express *different* partner preferences because reproduction is not an issue (Waynforth and Dunbar, 1995).

Maintenance

Stability
General factors that contribute to stability in gay and lesbian relationships include:
- For lesbian couples, equitable balance of power, high degree of emotional intimacy and high self-esteem (Eldridge and Gilbert, 1990).

- For gay couples, minimal conflict, high appreciation of the partner and co-operation (Jones and Bates, 1978).

Communication
Lesbian couples tend to use conversation to establish and maintain intimacy, whereas gay men use it as a means of asserting themselves (Huston and Schwartz, 1995).

Patterns of sexual behaviour
In gay and lesbian relationships these reflect the socialisation differences between the two sexes, with gay males typically being seen as more sexually promiscuous (Huston and Schwartz, 1995).

A conclusion is ... the way in which one partner uses communication may reflect the degree of power they have in the relationship.

However ... sexual infidelity may be a product of the relative lack of social convention for sexual behaviour among homosexual couples.

Dissolution

Differences between homosexual and heterosexual relationships
Gay and lesbian relationships do not appear to be as durable as heterosexual relationships (Blumstein and Schwartz, 1983), but gay and lesbian partners are more likely to remain friends after a sexual relationship has ended (Nardi, 1992).

Reasons for dissolution in gay and lesbian relationships
- Lesbian relationships often break up because one partner has an affair and falls in love with another woman.

- Gay relationships typically break up because of irresolvable power differences between the partners.

However ... although many of the *reasons* for dissolution are the same for heterosexual and homosexual couples, the *process* is more public for the former and more private for the latter.

General difficulties with gay and lesbian research
There are methodological (e.g. the difficulty of obtaining a representative sample) and ethical (i.e. this is a socially sensitive research) problems associated with research in this area.

Probable questions
1. Discuss research (theories **and/or** studies) into **two** types of understudied relationship.   *(24 marks)*
2. Discuss research (theories **and/or** studies) into understudied relationships.   *(24 marks)*

Possible questions
3. Discuss research (theories **and/or** studies) into **one** type of understudied relationship.   *(24 marks)*

Chapter 1
Social psychology
Relationships   >

Attraction and formation
Love and breakdown
Cultural and subcultural differences >

Relationships in different cultures (explanations)
Relationships in different cultures (studies)
Understudied relationships (gay and lesbian)
Understudied relationships (electronic)

Computer-mediated communication (CMC)

Development of Internet relationships
- **Initial attraction** Because bodily information is removed in CMC, text and text-related issues (e.g. frequency of e-mail contact) take on greater importance.

- **Finding love** Research (e.g. Chenault, 1998) shows that people in Internet relationships might have quite different perceptions of the *nature* of their relationship.

The nature of Internet relationships
- **Reduced cues** Reduced cues theory (Culnan and Markus, 1987) claims that CMC filters out important aspects of communication (e.g. intensity and volume) that are present in face-to-face relationships.

- **Deindividuation** A lack of physical and social cues in CMC leads to deindividuation (a lack of individual identity) which may in turn foster anti-normative and uninhibited behaviours.

However ... research support concerning the success of online relationships tends to be sparse. Most evidence comes from anecdotal accounts or magazine articles rather than properly controlled scientific studies.

Advantages of online relationships
- They are good for people who lack the skills or opportunities to develop face-to-face relationships.

- The *ACE model* (Young, 1999) – CMC offers *anonymity*, *convenience* and *escape*.

- CMC offers a way of 'getting to know' friends better compared with many friendships made in 'real life'.

Disadvantages of online relationships
Because individuals are able to control their self-representation, this can lead to deception and abuse. As a result, it is more difficult to develop trust between partners.

The SIDE model
This model counters the view that CMC liberates individuals from social constraints and norms. Although anonymity in CMC deprives individuals of *individual* identity awareness, a social or a *group* identity replaces it. This can then lead to the formation of strong relationships within groups on the Internet.

The role of the mobile telephone

Relational functions of mobile telephones
Mobile phones have changed the ways in which people develop and maintain relationships.
- **Co-ordination** Mobile phones allow family members to co-ordinate their activities and allow non-custodial parents to maintain contact with their children.

- **Parental control** Children can develop and maintain relationships without the parental control evident in other relationships.

- **Emancipation** Mobile phones facilitate emancipation from the family to 'adult' reference groups.

Development and maintenance of relationships through SMS messaging
This has an important role in the formation and maintenance of relationships.
- **Relationship formation** Texting can provide a 'contact ritual' whereby people can exchange messages after an initial meeting and thus show interest.

- **Relationship maintenance** Texting can be used to 'manage' relationships in the most efficient way, and may also be used to consolidate a social network.

Supported by ... Ling and Yttri (2002) who found that adolescents frequently exchange texts following an initial meeting. This allows them to register their interest in developing a relationship with the other person.

Advantage of SMS over CMC
- The immediacy of text messaging means that the mobile phone is a more efficient and convenient way of maintaining relationships than e-mail or other forms of communication.

- The use of SMS messaging means that we are always 'available', making it easier to co-ordinate the activities of a group of friends.

Disadvantages of mediated relationships
- Individuals may become overly reliant on CMC and SMS for the initiation and maintenance of relationships at the expense of face-to-face relationship skills.

- Because it is easier to send a text rather than visit in person, this can weaken face-to-face ties between individuals.

Probable and possible questions

See previous page

hapter 2	Nature and causes of aggression >	**Social–psychological theories of aggression**
ocial psychology	Altruism and bystander behaviour	Effects of environmental stressors on aggression
ro- and anti-social behaviour >	Media influences	

Theory 1: Social learning theory (SLT)   (BANDURA, 1963)

In a nutshell – SLT suggests that we learn the specifics of aggressive behaviour (the forms it takes and the targets toward which it is directed) by observing others.

The processes of social learning
How is aggressive behaviour *learned*?

- **Observation** Children learn aggressive behaviour by watching and imitating role models. They also learn the *consequences* of aggressive behaviour through vicarious reinforcement.

- **Mental representation** Children form mental representations of events in their social environment, together with expectancies of the likely outcomes of aggressive behaviour.

Production of behaviour
Under what circumstances is aggressive behaviour *produced*?

- **Maintenance through direct experience** A child may be directly reinforced for aggressive behaviour, which increases the value of aggressive behaviour for that child.

- **Self-efficacy expectancies** Children vary in the degree to which they have confidence in their ability to carry out aggressive actions successfully.

Supported by ... Bandura and Walters (1963), who found that children who watched an adult being rewarded for behaving aggressively showed a high level of imitative aggression later.

This shows that ... aggressive behaviour is encouraged by reward and discouraged by punishment.

Supported by ... Bandura (1965), who found that children who were given a reward for performing a model's aggressive behaviour were all able to reproduce that behaviour.

This shows that ... learning occurs regardless of reinforcement, but *production* of a behaviour is related to selective reinforcement.

Strengths
SLT can explain differences *between* individuals (i.e. cultural variation) and *within* individuals (selective reinforcement and context-dependent learning).

Limitations
SLT is not a complete explanation of aggression because it does not explain the *impulse* to aggress.

Theory 2: Deindividuation   (ZIMBARDO, 1969)

In a nutshell – A state of deindividuation arises when people lose their sense of individuality, leading to reduced self-restraint and an increase in deviant and impulsive behaviour.

Individuated and deindividuated behaviour
People refrain from aggressive behaviour because of social norms and risk of identification. In a crowd, anonymity reduces these restraints and increases behaviours that are usually inhibited.

The faceless crowd
Being part of a crowd can diminish both awareness of individuality and fear of negative evaluation of our actions.

Reduced private self-awareness
Recent formulations of deindividuation theory focus on the importance of reduced *private* self-awareness (becoming less self-aware) rather than reduced *public* self-awareness (simply being anonymous to others).

Research support ... for deindividuation comes from Haney *et al.*'s (1973) prison simulation study and Zimbardo's (1969) laboratory study.

Normative rather than anti-normative
Postmes and Spears' meta-analysis (1998) showed that deindividuation doesn't always lead to anti-normative behaviour, but may lead to increase in *compliance*.

This can be applied to ... an explanation of aggression in football crowds. Experiments have shown that aggression is reduced using mirrors and video cameras: this increases private self-awareness.

Probable questions
1. Outline and evaluate **two** social–psychological theories of aggression. (24 marks)
2. (a) Outline **two** social–psychological theories of aggression. (12 marks)
   (b) Evaluate the **two** social–psychological theories that you outlined in (a). (12 marks)

Possible questions
3. Describe and evaluate **one** social–psychological theory of aggression. (24 marks)

Chapter 2
Social psychology
Pro- and anti-social behaviour   >
Nature and causes of aggression   >
Altruism and bystander behaviour
Media influences
Social–psychological theories of aggression
Effects of environmental stressors on aggression

Stressor 1: Temperature

Explaining the relationship
- **Indirect links** (*Routine activity theory*) People behave differently in summer (outside more, more alcohol consumed) and thus beome more aggressive.

- **Direct links** (*Negative affect escape theory*) Negative affect increases with temperature. At high heat levels, aggression occurs if escape is not possible.

Research studies
- **Heat and frustration** (Kenrick and Macfarlane, 1986) Drivers responded more aggressively to frustration when heat levels were high.

- **Heat and violent crime** (Anderson, 1987) Archival records show violent crimes are more common in hotter years and hotter quarters of the year.

However ... although this 'indirect' explanation can explain naturalistic studies, it does not explain laboratory studies that show temperature as a causal factor.

However ... some studies show a curvilinear relationship between heat and aggression, but others (e.g. Anderson and Anderson, 1984) haven't found a decline in aggression at *very* high temperatures.

Alternatively ... the relationship could be biological, as heat activates the ANS and causes increased testosterone, leading to aggression.

Limitations
- Naturalistic studies provide only correlational data.

- Other variables that may lead to aggression are uncontrolled.

Stressor 2: Noise

Explaining the relationship
Noise alone is not believed to cause aggression, but when combined with pre-existing anger, may trigger aggressive behaviour.

Research studies
- **Laboratory studies** Geen and O'Neal (1969) found that loud noise increases aggressiveness; Donnerstein and Wilson (1976) found that levels of aggression decrease if people believe they have some control over noise.

- **Exposure to aircraft noise** Evans *et al.* (1998) found that long-term exposure to aircraft noise caused increases in blood pressure and stress hormones in children.

This can be understood by ... seeing noise as being like any other stressor. It increases ANS activity, and predisposes people to aggressive behaviour.

This can be explained by ... the fact that aircraft noise may cause *tiredness*, which was what caused children to behave aggressively, rather than the noise itself.

Stressor 3: Crowding

Explaining the relationship
Crowding may create arousal (and hence aggression) because of insufficient personal space and diminished sense of control.

Research studies
- **Crowding and violent crime** Some studies found a positive correlation between high population density and violent crime (Schmitt, 1967).

- **Crowding on the dance floor** A study of nightclubs found that level of crowding was related to the number of aggressive incidents (Macintyre and Hornel, 1997).

A problem is that ... the effects of crowding vary with social context (see *Deindividuation*, page 11).

However ... this relationship disappears when other social factors are controlled (Freedman, 1975).

Probable questions
1. Describe and evaluate research (explanations **and/or** studies) into the effects of **two or more** environmental stressors on behaviour.

(24 marks)

Possible questions
2. Describe and evaluate research (explanations **and/or** studies) into the effects of **two** environmental stressors on behaviour.

(24 marks)

Chapter 2 | Nature and causes of aggression > | **Altruism/bystander behaviour (explanations)**
Social psychology | Altruism and bystander behaviour > | Altruism/bystander behaviour (studies)
Pro- and anti-social behaviour > | Media influences | Cultural differences in pro-social behaviour

Explanation 1: The empathy–altruism hypothesis (BATSON, 1991)

In a nutshell – Explanations differ in terms of whether they see altruism as *selfless* or *selfish* behaviour.

Empathy
This involves feeling an emotional response that is consistent with another's emotional state.

Perspective-taking
Witnessing someone in need only leads to empathetic concern if the observer takes the perspective of that person.

Helping Elaine
Participants in the high empathy condition still helped even when given the opportunity to leave (Batson *et al.*, 1981).

Oneness or empathy?
Cialdini *et al.* (1997) claimed 'oneness' (closeness of association) was a better indicator of helping than empathetic concern.

However ... Batson *et al.* (1997) found that oneness did not affect helping.

Learned or biological?
Kin selection theory states that we are likely to help those with whom we share genes.

This is supported by ... research (e.g. Kruger, 2003).

Limitations
Altruistic concern for others can easily be crushed by experimental manipulations where participants' attention is turned toward themselves (Batson *et al.*, 1983).

However ... it is possible that participants in Batson's study saw through the deception and acted accordingly.

This study has external validity ... as Oliner and Oliner (1988) found that 37% of those who helped Jews during World War II did so for altruistic reasons.

Explanation 2: The decision model (LATANÉ AND DARLEY, 1970)

In a nutshell – This model explains why bystanders sometimes *do* and sometimes *don't* offer help in an emergency.

Five-stage model
Before bystanders intervene, they must:
1 notice the situation
2 interpret it as an emergency
3 accept personal responsibility to intervene
4 consider what is the best form of intervention
5 decide how to implement the intervention.

Psychological processes
- **Diffusion of responsibility** The more witnesses, the more responsibility is shared.
- **Pluralistic ignorance** If others fail to help, the situation may not be interpreted as an emergency.

Research support includes:
Stage 2: In an ambiguous situation, people are less likely to help (Clark and Word, 1972).
Stage 3: Studies of diffusion of responsibility and pluralistic ignorance (e.g. Darley *et al.*, 1973).
Stage 4: Bystanders trained in first aid are more likely to help (Cramer *et al.*, 1988).

Diffusion of responsibility is supported by ... Latané and Dabbs (1975), who found that the probability of helping decreased with the number of bystanders.

Pluralistic ignorance is supported by ... (Darley *et al.*, 1973), who found that this tendency was greater when bystanders were unable to see each other's facial expressions.

Limitations of the model
- It takes no account of *impulsive* behaviour.
- In real-life emergencies the cost of *not* helping is high, so people are inclined to help.
- People may also help because of *personal norms*.

This has been applied by ... Cialdini (1985), who found that in order to elicit help in an emergency, it is necessary to remove the situational factors that inhibit helping.

Probable questions
1. Outline and evaluate **two** explanations of human altruism **and/or** bystander behaviour. *(24 marks)*

Possible questions
2. Discuss research (explanations **and/or** research studies) relating to human altruism **and/or** bystander behaviour. *(24 marks)*

Chapter 2
Social psychology
Pro- and anti-social behaviour >

Nature and causes of aggression
Altruism and bystander behaviour >
Media influences

Altruism/bystander behaviour (explanations)
Altruism/bystander behaviour (studies)
Cultural differences in pro-social behaviour

Study 1: Helping Elaine
Participants in the high empathy condition still helped even when given the opportunity to leave (Batson et al., 1981).

This suggests that ... people help for reasons other than just the reduction of their own personal distress.

However ... it is possible that participants in Batson et al.'s study saw through the deception and acted accordingly.

Study 2: Gaining social approval
Fultz et al. (1986) found that the possibility of social evaluation did not increase helping in a high empathy condition, whereas in a low empathy condition helping was lower if there was no possibility of social evaluation.

This suggests that ... when empathy is aroused, people are likely to help for purely altruistic reasons, but in the absence of empathy, egoistic reasons are more important in determining whether help will be given.

In real life people may behave differently ... according to Oliner and Oliner (1988), who found that 37% of those who helped Jews during World War II did so for altruistic reasons.

Study 3: What determines altruistic behaviour?
Kruger (2003) found that genetic relatedness and reciprocity (egoistic factors) were more important than empathy in determining the likelihood of performing a risky rescue behaviour.

This shows that ... although empathy may influence altruistic behaviour, it does so within a more selfishly motivated system where reciprocity and genetic relatedness are more important.

However ... research may have exaggerated the differences between Western and non-Western cultures in that most research on altruism has focused on the attitudes and experiences of *students*, who represent a biased sample.

Studies 4: Related to the decision model
- **Stage 2** In an ambiguous situation, people are less likely to help (Clark and Word, 1972).
- **Stage 3** Studies of diffusion of responsibility and pluralistic ignorance (e.g. Darley et al., 1973).
- **Stage 4** Bystanders trained in first aid are more likely to help (Cramer et al., 1988).

One problem is ... that such studies sometimes lacked mundane realism.

However ... the decision model assumes that we think rationally.

It does not explain ... what motivates helping, but this can be explained with reference to personal norms (Schwartz and Howard, 1981).

Studies 5: Diffusion of responsibility
- Latané and Dabbs (1975) found that the probability of helping decreased with the number of bystanders present.
- Latané and Darley (1970) found that people were more likely to offer help to someone who had dropped books in a lift if *one* other person was present than if *six* other people present.

A conclusion is that ... field studies have generally found that people are more helpful than is the case in laboratory studies.

However ... not all studies carried out in natural settings have found that larger numbers of bystanders means less help is given.

Probable questions
1. (a) Outline **two** explanations of human altruism **and/or** bystander behaviour. (12 marks)
   (b) Evaluate the **two** explanations of human altruism that you outlined in (a) in terms of relevant research studies. (12 marks)
2. Discuss **two or more** research studies relating to human altruism **and/or** bystander behaviour. (24 marks)

Possible questions
3. Discuss research (explanations **and/or** research studies) relating to human altruism **and/or** bystander behaviour. (24 marks)

Chapter 2
Social psychology
Pro- and anti-social behaviour >

Nature and causes of aggression
Altruism and bystander behaviour >
Media influences

Altruism/bystander behaviour (explanations)
Altruism/bystander behaviour (studies)
Cultural differences in pro-social behaviour

Subcultural differences

In a nutshell – Subcultural groups share many of the dominant cultural characteristics of that society, but also have special characteristics.

Gender differences
Females display greater empathy (Eisenberg and Lennon, 1983) and more pronounced feelings of guilt (Bybee, 1998). Men are more likely to intervene in an emergency (Eagly and Crowley, 1986).

Urban–rural differences
A study in Turkey found that helpfulness was higher for people in small towns than in large cities (Korte and Ayvalioglu, 1981).

Information overload (Milgram, 1970)
Urban dwellers deal with high levels of stimulation by screening out less personally relevant information, so becoming indifferent to the needs of others.

Gender differences can be explained by ... evolved characteristics of the two sexes, or by the influence of gender stereotypes.

In contrast to ... the gender stereotype that women are more helpful than men, a meta-analysis found that men were actually more helpful than women (Eagly and Crowley, 1986).

Supported by ... a meta-analysis of many different cultures that also found that more help was offered in rural than urban areas (Steblay, 1987).

Alternative explanations suggest that ... urban societies are also more competitive, with assertiveness more important than helping.

This would explain ... why people *appear* indifferent to the needs of those in distress.

Cultural variations

In a nutshell – Western cultures are *individualist*, valuing independence rather than reliance on others. Non-Western cultures are *collectivist*, valuing interdependence.

Individualist versus collectivist societies
• **Cultural norms** Collectivist cultures have a *duty-based* view of interpersonal responsibilities; individualist cultures have a more *option-based* perspective (Miller, 1994).

• **Assigning responsibility** In individualist cultures transgressions usually attributed to the individual wrong-doer. In collectivist cultures, the social context is considered and help is more forthcoming.

Research studies of kibbutzim children show that they are more co-operative and helpful than their American and European peers (Moghaddam et al., 1993). Research in collectivist cultures (e.g. native American, Polynesian, Maori) found pronounced patterns of pro-social behaviour (Mann, 1980).

Meaning of pro-social behaviour in different cultures
Some cultures see foreigners as being more important and worthy of help (Collett and O'Shea, 1976).

However ... within collectivist societies, different subcultures may differ in terms of pro-social behaviour (e.g. Merchant's 2001 study of Indian Muslim and Hindu students). Collectivist cultures also tend to be more rural, which may contribute to their more pro-social nature.

Limitations of research methodology
• Pro-social behaviour is affected by context, so lab studies may miss the *social* function of helping.
• Samples studied (frequently students) may not represent the *whole* culture.

Also ... a helpful act may have meaning beyond just providing assistance, e.g. establishing power and creating indebtedness (e.g. Chinese system of *guanxixue*).

However ... in Western cultures, the notion of 'networking' also involves limited obligations among individuals concerning mutual help.

Probable questions

1. Discuss research (theories **and/or** studies) relating to cultural differences in pro-social behaviour. *(24 marks)*

2. (a) Outline **one or more** explanations of human altruism **and/or** bystander behaviour. *(12 marks)*

   (b) To what extent are there cultural differences in pro-social behaviour? *(12 marks)*

Possible questions

3. Outline **two or more** aspects of pro-social behaviour in which there are cultural differences. *(24 marks)*

Chapter 2	Nature and causes of aggression	**Pro-social behaviour (explanations)**
Social psychology	Altruism and bystander behaviour	Pro-social behaviour (studies)
Pro- and anti-social behaviour >		Anti-social behaviour (explanations)
	Media influences >	Anti-social behaviour (studies)

Explanation 1: Exposure to pro-social behaviour

Content
Despite concern over the *anti-social* content in popular television programmes, there is clear evidence of a comparable level of *pro-social* content (Greenberg *et al.*, 1980).

Relative effects
These pro-social acts frequently appear alongside acts of anti-social behaviour which may explain why their influence tends to be overshadowed.

Supported by ... Woodard (1999), who found that 77% of children's programmes in the US contained pro-social messages, but only 4 of the top 20 most-watched programmes did so.

Effectiveness of pro-social programming
Prolonged viewing of pro-social programmes can result in substantial increases in children's pro-social reasoning (Eisenberg, 1983).

Explanation 2: Acquisition of pro-social behaviours and norms

Observational learning
Bandura (1965) argues that children learn by *observing* behaviour, and imitating those behaviours that are likely to bring rewards.

Pro-social acts represent social norms
Unlike the depiction of anti-social acts, pro-social acts tend to *represent* social norms rather than *contrast* with them. Children are more likely to be rewarded for imitating pro-social acts.

However ... children are most affected by pro-social messages when *concrete* pro-social acts are demonstrated rather than more abstract messages.

Pro-social versus anti-social effects
Children are able to generalise better from watching anti-social rather than pro-social acts on TV. Mixing the two together may have a damaging effect on any pro-social message (Silverman and Sprafkin, 1980).

Explanation 3: Developmental factors

Reasoning skills
Reasoning skills synonymous with pro-social behaviour (e.g. empathy) develop throughout childhood and into adolescence; therefore young children are less likely to be affected by pro-social messages.

Ability to understand pro-social messages
Research suggests that young children have more difficulty understanding abstract pro-social messages in TV programmes and so may be less affected by them.

However ... Mares (1996) found that the weakest effect from pro-social programming was on adolescents, and strongest on primary school children.

This might be explained by ... the fact that young children may imitate pro-social acts if they believe they will bring a reward. Adolescents may act pro-socially for purely altruistic reasons.

Probable questions
1. Discuss explanations relating to media influences on pro-social behaviour. *(24 marks)*

Possible questions
2. (a) Outline **two or more** explanations relating to media influences on pro-social behaviour. *(12 marks)*

   (b) Evaluate the **two or more** explanations relating to media influences on pro-social behaviour in terms of relevant research studies. *(12 marks)*

apter 2

cial psychology

ro- and anti-social behaviour >

Nature and causes of aggression	Pro-social behaviour (explanations)
Altruism and bystander behaviour	**Pro-social behaviour (studies)**
Media influences >	Anti-social behaviour (explanations)
	Anti-social behaviour (studies)

Study 1: Hearold (1986) carried out meta-analysis of over 200 studies of the effects of TV and found that pro-social themes had a greater effect on pro-social behaviour than did anti-social themes on anti-social behaviour.

However ... Comstock (1989) claims that Hearold's findings are due to the fact that pro-social programmes are generally designed to give pro-social messages, whereas anti-social programmes are not designed to give anti-social messages.

Study 2: Mares (1996) examined all available research published between 1966 and 1995, considering four main behavioural effects of pro-social TV: altruism, positive interaction, self-control and anti-stereotyping.

Gender differences
Mares found significant gender differences in pro-social effects, with more positive effects evident for girls than boys.

This contrasts with ... the findings of Hearold (1986), who found that the effects of pro-social TV were consistently higher for girls *and* boys, although stronger for girls after the age of 6.

Study 3: Altruism (e.g. sharing, offering help, comforting)
Children who saw pro-social content (episode of Lassie) behaved more altruistically than those who viewed neutral or anti-social content (Poulos *et al.*, 1975).

Study 4: Positive interaction (e.g. friendly interactions, peaceable conflict resolution)
Friedrich and Stein (1973) found that children who watched a pro-social programme behaved more positively towards each other than those who had watched a neutral programme.

Problems with interpretation
• Behaviour was usually measured shortly after viewing, rather than testing for long-term effects.
• When more *generalised* pro-social behaviours are measured, the effect is smaller.

Study 5: Self-control (e.g. resistance to temptation, obedience to rules, task persistence)
Children exposed to a pro-social programme later showed higher levels of self-control in their own behaviour (Friedrich and Stein, 1973).

Subcultural individual differences
The socioeconomic background of children influenced their receptiveness to these messages, but this difference was only short-lived.

Study 6: Anti-stereotyping (e.g. counter-stereotypes of gender and ethnic groups)
Johnston and Ettema (1982) found that children become less stereotyped or prejudiced after watching an anti sex-role stereotyping programme.

However ... other research (e.g. Pingree, 1978) has found that boys displayed *stronger* sex-role stereotypes after viewing non-traditional models.

Probable questions

1. Discuss research (explanations **and/or** research studies) relating to media influences on pro-social behaviour. *(24 marks)*

2. (a) Outline and evaluate **two or more** explanations relating to media influences on pro-social behaviour. *(12 marks)*

   (b) Outline and evaluate **two or more** research studies relating to media influences on pro-social behaviour. *(12 marks)*

Possible questions

3. (a) Outline **two or more** research studies relating to media influences on pro-social behaviour. *(12 marks)*

   (b) Evaluate the **two or more** research studies relating to media influences on pro-social behaviour in terms of relevant research studies. *(12 marks)*

4. Critically consider explanations **and** research studies relating to media influences on pro-social behaviour. *(24 marks)*

Chapter 2	Nature and causes of aggression	Pro-social behaviour (explanations)
Social psychology	Altruism and bystander behaviour	Pro-social behaviour (research)
Pro- and anti-social behaviour >	Media influences >	**Anti-social behaviour (explanations)**
		Anti-social behaviour (research)

Huesmann and Moise (1996) suggest five ways in which exposure to media violence might lead to aggression.

Explanation 1: Observational learning

- Bandura (1986) claims that TV can teach skills that may be used when committing acts of violence.
- Children observe actions of media models and may later imitate these actions, especially if they identify with the model and the model's anti-social behaviour is rewarded.

Supported by ... Felson (1999), who provides research evidence that exposure to TV violence has an effect on some viewers through social learning.

However ... although observational learning from violent films has been demonstrated in the lab, evidence from real-life scenarios is quite rare and claims are often unsubstantiated.

Explanation 2: Cognitive priming

- Aggressive media may trigger a network of memories involving aggression and so predispose the viewer to act in an aggressive manner.
- Children may store aggressive scripts that they recall later if any aspect of the original situation is present.

Supported by ... Josephson (1987) who found evidence of cognitive priming among ice hockey players following exposure to a violent film.

This might explain ... why the observation of aggression is often followed by aggressive acts that differ from the observed behaviour (Huesmann, 2001).

Explanation 3: Desensitisation

Under normal conditions anxiety about aggression inhibits its use. Frequent viewing of media violence desensitises viewers to its effects and represents violence as 'normal'.

However ... Cumberbatch (2001) argues that although children may get 'used' to screen violence, it does not follow that they would also get used to violence in the real world.

Explanation 4: Physiological arousal

Frequent viewing of media violence leads to less physiological arousal as a result of viewing violent behaviour and thus fewer inhibitions concerning its use.

Supported by ... Cline et al. (1973) who found that boys who regularly watched violent TV showed less physiological arousal to violence.

Alternative effects such as ... watching violence may *increase* aggressiveness (Zillman's excitation transfer model, 1988) or release pent-up energy (catharsis) and therefore *decrease* it.

Explanation 5: Justification

- Under normal circumstances, aggressive behaviour should lead to feelings of guilt.
- Television may provide a justification for an individual's violent behaviour. As a result, guilt and concern about consequences of violence diminish, as do inhibitions about future aggression.

Supported by ... Anderson and Dill's (2000) study which showed that people who were initially more aggressive were more affected (i.e became more aggressive) by playing violent computer games.

This means that ... the negative effects of mixed pro- and anti-social messages might be explained in terms of the 'good guys' having moral justification for their violence.

Probable questions

1. Discuss explanations relating to media influences on anti-social behaviour. *(24 marks)*

Possible questions

2. (a) Outline **two or more** explanations relating to media influences on anti-social behaviour. *(12 marks)*

   (b) Evaluate the **two or more** explanations relating to media influences on anti-social behaviour in terms of relevant research studies. *(12 marks)*

apter 2
cial psychology
ro- and anti-social behaviour >

Nature and causes of aggression
Altruism and bystander behaviour
Media influences >

Pro-social behaviour (explanations)
Pro-social behaviour (studies)
Anti-social behaviour (explanations)

Anti-social behaviour (studies)

As well as individual studies of anti-social effects, *meta-analyses* (e.g. Paik and Comstock, 1994) offer a more global view of research in this area.

Study 1: The National Television Violence (1994–1997)
Researchers evaluated 10,000 hours of TV, and found the highest proportion of violence in children's programmes, which also showed fewest long-term negative consequences of violence.

The anti-effects lobby
- Belson (1978) found that boys who watched the *most* violent television were half as aggressive as those who watched moderate amounts (suggesting that the relationship is unpredictable).
- Hagell and Newburn (1994) found that violent teenage offenders watched *less* TV than non-offenders.

Study 2: Meta-analysis of research (PAIK AND COMSTOCK, 1994)
- The researchers examined 217 studies and found a highly significant relationship between television violence and aggressive behaviour, which was slightly higher in males.
- The size of the relationship depended on the age of participant and the genre of programming.

Limitation
Many of the earlier studies were laboratory-based, i.e. not typical of a child's normal television experience.

However ... in response to claims that correlations were quite small, Bushman and Anderson (2001) point out that they were second only to the relationship between smoking and lung cancer.

Study 3: St Helena (CHARLTON ET AL., 2000)
- The vast majority of measures used to assess pro- and anti-social behaviour showed no difference in either after introduction of television.
- The high levels of good behaviour noted before TV's arrival continued *despite* the same level of violence in films as that shown in the US.

However ... other natural experiments *have* found a difference after the introduction of TV (e.g. Williams, 1986).

This can be explained by ... Charlton who suggests that a strong community identity removed the need to be aggressive in St Helena.

Studies 4: Video games and aggression
- **Dill and Dill (1998)** A recent review of research evidence in this area concluded that exposure to video game violence increases aggressive behaviour.
- **Anderson and Bushman (2001)** A meta-analysis of 33 studies found a small but significant correlation between exposure to violence during game play and subsequent aggressive behaviour.

Limitations
- Most studies in this area have been correlational, and do not indicate a *causal* relationship between playing violent video games and violence behaviour.
- Studies rarely distinguish between aggressive *behaviour* and aggressive *play*, which may lead to faulty conclusions.

Probable questions
1. Discuss research (explanations **and/or** research studies) relating to media influences on anti-social behaviour. *(24 marks)*
2. (a) Outline and evaluate **two or more** explanations relating to media influences on anti-social behaviour. *(12 marks)*
   (b) Outline and evaluate **two or more** research studies relating to media influences on anti-social behaviour. *(12 marks)*

Possible questions
3. (a) Outline **two or more** research studies relating to media influences on anti-social behaviour. *(12 marks)*
   (b) Evaluate the **two or more** research studies relating to media influences on anti-social behaviour in terms of relevant research studies. *(12 marks)*
4. Critically consider explanations **and** research studies relating to media influences on anti-social behaviour. *(24 marks)*

Chapter 3	Biological rhythms >	Circadian, infradian and ultradian rhythms
Physiological psychology	Sleep	Endogenous pacemakers, exogenous zeitgebers
Biological rhythms, sleep, dreams >	Dreams	Consequences of disrupting rhythms

Circadian rhythms

Circadian rhythms last for 24 hours.

Sleep–wake cycle
- **Endogenous evidence** from isolation studies, e.g. Siffre (1975) lived in a cave for 6 months; his rhythm varied between 24 and 48 hours.
- **Exogenous zeitgebers** Bright light resets circadian rhythm; dim light may have an effect too (Wever et al., 1983).

Temperature cycle
This is highest at 4 p.m.; certain cognitive behaviours vary with the temperature, e.g. memory (Folkard et al., 1977).

However ... in isolation studies, participants are not isolated from artificial light; therefore they are not actually testing the free running cycle.

Research suggests **individual differences** in sleep–wake cycle length (Czeisler et al., 1999) and cycle onset (Duffy et al., 2000).

Exogenous zeitgebers are important because ... they enable circadian rhythms to synchronise with the environment.

However ... temperature rhythm is different from sleep–wake rhythm, suggesting more than one biological clock.

Applications include ... chronotherapy and the importance of timing in medical tests.

Infradian rhythms

Infradian rhythms have a period greater than 24 hours but less than 1 year.

Monthly cycles
- The human menstrual cycle is on average 29.5 days.
- There is a male cycle affecting temperature and mood which lasts 20 days (Empson, 1977).

Seasonal affective disorder (SAD)
- Sufferers are depressed in winter.
- Melatonin (related to depression) is higher in winter.

Research support
Synchronisation of menstrual cycles in women living together, i.e. influence of exogenous zeitgebers – social cues transmitted through pheromones (Russell et al., 1980).

However ... despite the implication that a pheromone is involved in this process, it has yet to be isolated.

Applications of this research include ... using the understanding of SAD to develop effective therapies such as phototherapy.

Ultradian rhythms

Ultradian rhythms span a period less than 1 day.

Sleep stages
- NREM sleep: stages 1 and 2 are relaxed; stages 3 and 4 are SWS (growth hormone released).
- REM sleep: dreams, neurotransmitters made.

Basic rest-activity cycle (BRAC)
- Friedman and Fisher (1967) gave evidence of cyclic eating and drinking behaviour.

However ... dreams are not exclusively linked to REM sleep; it is possible to explain dreaming in terms of a psychological rather than neurobiological function.

A limitation of this research is that ... sleep stages are recorded in artificial laboratory studies.

Research support
BRAC is generally supported by research studies, e.g. Grau et al. (1995), who confirmed the existence of an ultradian rhythm in motor activity in humans.

Probable questions
1. Describe and evaluate research into **one** biological rhythm (e.g. circadian, infradian, ultradian). *(24 marks)*
2. Outline and evaluate research into **two or more** biological rhythms. *(24 marks)*

Possible questions
3. Discuss research into circadian rhythms. *(24 marks)*
4. (a) Critically consider research into infradian rhythms. *(12 marks)*
   (b) Critically consider research into ultradian rhythms. *(12 marks)*

Chapter 3

Physiological psychology

Biological rhythms, sleep, dreams

Biological rhythms	>	Circadian, infradian and ultradian rhythms
Sleep		**Endogenous pacemakers, exogenous zeitgebers**
Dreams		Consequences of disrupting rhythms

Endogenous pacemaker

An endogenous pacemaker is an internal biological clock that controls an organism's circadian rhythms.

Biological clock
- This is created by interactions between proteins CLOCK and CYCLE, and PER and TIM.
- They work in a feedback loop.

Suprachiasmatic nucleus (SCN)
- This is found In the hypothalamus and obtains information about light from the optic nerve.
- It depends on light to synchronise the biological clock with the cycles of light and dark in the outside world.

Pineal gland
- The pineal gland responds when light increases by inhibiting the production of melatonin (which is responsible for inducing sleep).
- It is an especially important pacemaker in birds and reptiles (the third eye).

Advantage of the biological clock
Without one, an animal may have irregular patterns of activity that may be life-threatening.

Disadvantage
Rhythms may not change as rapidly as we need (e.g. effects of shiftwork, jet lag).

Evidence for the importance of the SCN
- If the SCN is damaged, the animal no longer responds to environmental cues, e.g. research with mutant hamsters (Morgan, 1995).
- Destruction of the SCN in chipmunks led to increased activity at night and a greater risk of predation (DeCoursey et al., 2000).

The importance of the pineal gland is shown by ...
the fact that after the removal of pineal gland, an animal may continue to produce melatonin (Moyer et al., 1997).

Research support
Chickens wake and become active as dawn breaks (when external light levels rise and melatonin levels fall) (Binkley, 1979).

Exogenous zeitgebers

These are environmental cues that reset the biological clock so that it matches local conditions.

Social cues
These include meal times and normal bed times. Until recently these were thought to be the main human zeitgeber.

Light
This is the dominant zeitgeber in humans. Bright light suppresses melatonin, but even dim lighting may have an effect (Wever et al., 1983).

Temperature
Temperature can also entrain biological rhythms; it causes leaves to drop and hibernation to commence.

However ... social cues are important only in social animals; the purpose is to provide a means of regulating social behaviours.

Importance of light as a zeitgeber
- It ensures activity during daylight and inactivity during darkness.
- Blind people experience difficulty maintaining a 24-hour cycle, e.g. one man had a rhythm of 24.9 hours despite clocks and other social cues (Miles et al., 1977).

However ... it is possible to override the biological system – people told to wake up earlier have raised hormone levels just before designated time – a case of mind over matter (Born et al., 1999).

Probable questions
1. Discuss the role of endogenous pacemakers and exogenous zeitgebers. *(24 marks)*

Possible questions
2. Describe and evaluate the role of endogenous pacemakers. *(24 marks)*
3. Describe and evaluate the role of exogenous zeitgebers. *(24 marks)*

Chapter 3
Physiological psychology
Biological rhythms, sleep, dreams >

Biological rhythms >
Sleep
Dreams

Circadian, infradian and ultradian rhythms
Endogenous pacemakers, exogenous zeitgebers
Consequences of disrupting rhythms

Shiftwork (shift lag)

In a nutshell – Disruption of the 24-hour circadian rhythm in nightworkers leads to a circadian 'trough' in alertness at about 6 a.m. (Boivin *et al.*, 1966).

Partial sleep deprivation
- Sleeping during the day is difficult because of daytime noises and light.
- Sleep is typically 1–2 hours shorter (Tilley and Wilkinson, 1982).
- REM is particularly affected.

Poor quality sleep
- Quantity and quality of sleep are affected.
- Sleep deficit and fatigue then affect work performance.

Heart disease
Shiftworkers are three times more likely to develop heart disease (Knutsson, 1982).

Individual differences in how people cope with shiftwork: those whose circadian rhythms are slowest to adapt cope better (Reinberg *et al.*, 1984).

Desynchronisation of different rhythms may cause problems
The sleep–wake cycle is quicker to adjust (48 hours) (Yamazaki *et al.*, 2000).

Rotating shifts have the most harmful effects
These can be minimised by rotating shifts in one direction, i.e. phase delay (Czeisler *et al.*, 1982).

Although ... dim lighting does not appear to reset the biological clock, bright lights can mimic the effect of daylight and reset the biological clock within 3 days (Czeisler *et al.*, 1986).

An application of this research is shown by ... Czeisler *et al.* (1982), who gave advice to a US company: worker satisfaction and output then increased.

Jet lag

In a nutshell – Jet lag is caused by the sudden creation of a large discrepancy between the internal clock and the external world.

Non-adaptive
The biological clock is not equipped to deal with sudden changes of time zone.

Travelling east to west
- Adjustment is more difficult when flying east to west (i.e. phase advance) because disruption of the circadian rhythm is more dramatic.
- Baseball teams won 37% of games when travelling west to east (phase advance) and 44% when travelling east to west (Recht *et al.*, 1995).

However ... other factors (e.g. anxiety, alcohol, low oxygen in cabin air) might also contribute to the harmful effects of jet lag.

Why is jet lag harmful?
Jet lag causes desynchronisation of body clocks throughout the body.

Research support
A BRE meta-study (2001) found evidence of reduced alertness and concentration related to jet lag.

However ... findings on mental performance were inconsistent, suggesting the role of motivation or some other confounding factor.

However ... studies of the effects of jet lag on athletes have been inconclusive, suggesting performance is not adversely affected provided motivation remains high.

Staying up late and getting up late

- This *subverts* established circadian rhythms.
- Sleeping longer has effects similar to sleeping less.

Research support
Participants slept either 9 p.m.–5 a.m. or 3 a.m.–11 a.m. Both groups showed reduced alertness and vigilance (Taub and Berger, 1976).

Probable questions
1. Discuss the consequences of disrupting biological rhythms (e.g. jet lag, shift work). (24 marks)
2. (a) Outline research into **one or more** biological rhythms. (12 marks)
   (b) Assess the consequences of disrupting such rhythms. (12 marks)

Possible questions
3. Critically consider the consequences of disrupting biological rhythms. (24 marks)

Chapter 3
Physiological psychology
Biological rhythms, sleep, dreams >

Biological rhythms
Sleep >
Dreams

Function of sleep: ecological (explanations)
Function of sleep: ecological (studies)
Function of sleep: restoration (explanations)
Function of sleep: restoration (studies)

In a nutshell – Sleep has an important adaptive value. Sleep conserves energy at times when food is scarce and enables animals to avoid predators.

Explanation 1: Energy conservation (WEBB, 1982)

Energy costs
Maintaining body temperature and having a high metabolic rate (chemical processes in body) have a physiological cost; foraging and escaping from predators also have an energy cost.

Energy conserved
Sleep is enforced inactivity (like hibernation).

Negative correlation
The amount of sleep is negatively correlated with body size. This relationship is further modified by foraging needs and predator danger.

Supported by ... Allison and Cicchetti (1976), who found that larger animals experience less NREM sleep but not less REM sleep, showing that only NREM sleep is important for energy conservation.

It may be that ...
- NREM sleep evolved first (reptiles don't have REM sleep) for energy conservation.
- REM sleep evolved later in animals with larger brains – to exercise neural circuits.

However ... energy conservation in sleep is minimal (5–10%) and the risks are large. Energy can be conserved by partial inactivity (e.g. unilateral sleep).

Explanation 2: Foraging requirements

Animals with higher metabolic rates
Such animals sleep for longer (Zepelin and Rechtschaffen, 1974).

Sleep duration
This is influenced by foraging requirements. Herbivores eat food low in nutrients and sleep little. Carnivores eat food rich in nutrients so sleep longer.

However ... despite this finding, some species (e.g. the sloth) contradict this trend.

This account offers an explanation for why ... there is so much variety in sleep patterns among species – they must adapt to the different pressures of their environments.

Explanation 3: Predator avoidance (MEDDIS, 1975)

Negative correlation
The amount of sleep taken by an animal correlates negatively with the amount of danger typically experienced (Allison and Cicchetti, 1976).

Prey species sleep less to be vigilant
- But if they have to sleep it is best to do so when they are least vulnerable, e.g. at night.
- It is best to stay still (i.e. sleep) when there is nothing better to do.

Unilateral sleep
Dolphins and some birds display unilateral sleep to maintain predator vigilance whilst conserving energy.

Disadvantages of sleep
Sleep is a costly behaviour as while asleep, animals cannot be vigilant against predators, forage or protect their young.

However ... it is possible that the greater 'stillness' of sleep renders prey species safer from predators than when simply resting.

However ... Boerema et al. (2003) found that sleep-deprived chickens slept with both halves of their brain at the cost of reduced alertness.

General commentary
Sleep does not appear to have significant advantages in terms of energy conservation and predator avoidance. It may have significant disadvantages.

Probable questions
1. Discuss **one or more** ecological theories of sleep. *(24 marks)*

Possible questions
2. (a) Describe the ecological account of sleep. *(12 marks)*
   (b) Evaluate the ecological account of sleep in terms of relevant research studies. *(12 marks)*

23

Chapter 3
Physiological psychology
Biological rhythms, sleep, dreams >

Biological rhythms
Sleep   >
Dreams

Function of sleep: ecological (explanations)
Function of sleep: ecological (studies)
Function of sleep: restoration (explanations)
Function of sleep: restoration (studies)

Study 1: Sleep length and energy conservation

There is a negative correlation between the body size of a species and the amount of time spent sleeping. Small animals (e.g. brown bats) spend more hours asleep than large animals (e.g. elephants) (Zepelin and Rechtschaffen, 1974).

This supports the claim that ... animals with higher metabolic rates need to conserve energy by sleeping for longer periods.

However ... Allison and Cicchetti (1976) found that larger animals experience less NREM sleep but not less REM sleep, showing that only NREM sleep is important for energy conservation.

Study 2: Endothermy and NREM sleep

- Research has provided evidence for the universal presence of NREM sleep in endothermic (warm-blooded) mammals and birds and its absence in reptiles and other ectothermic (cold-blooded) species.
- NREM sleep is seen to have evolved as a way of conserving the energy needed to maintain endothermy.

However ... Kavanau (2004) claims that the loss of muscle tone associated with NREM sleep would have been insufficient to prevent muscle contractions during sleep.

Study 3: Sleep length and predator avoidance

Allison and Cicchetti (1976) found that the more danger typically faced by a species, the less it slept.

This supports the claims that ...
- Evolution of sleep is associated with the need to remain safe from predators.
- Large amounts of REM sleep are disadvantageous to prey species.

However ... data are correlational, i.e. do not demonstrate a causal relationship.

Also ... the inverse relationship between sleep and predator avoidance does not hold true for all animals, e.g. rabbits (high danger) sleep the same as moles (low danger rating).

Study 4: Unilateral sleep

- Birds watching for predators keep one eye open and corresponding hemisphere active (Rattenborg et al., 1999).
- Mukhametov (1984) found that bottlenose dolphins 'switch off' one hemisphere at a time. During sleep they are still able to come up to the surface to breathe.

This shows that ... marine mammals are able to gain the benefits of sleep while at the same time avoiding dangers in their environment.

However ... Boerema et al. (2003) found that other birds (e.g. chickens) abandon unilateral sleep when sleep-deprived at the cost of reduced alertness.

Study 5: REM sleep and developmental complexity

Zepelin (1989) has shown that altricial animals (unable to care for themselves) have much larger amounts of REM sleep at birth than precocial mammals, with immaturity at birth the single best predictor of REM sleep time throughout life.

This suggests that ... there is a link between the need for REM sleep and greater developmental complexity.

Probable questions

1. Discuss **two or more** research studies relating to the ecological account of sleep. *(24 marks)*

2. (a) Outline the ecological account of sleep. *(6 marks)*

   (b) Discuss research studies relating to the ecological account of sleep. *(18 marks)*

Possible questions

3. (a) Describe the ecological account of sleep. *(12 marks)*

   (b) Evaluate the ecological account of sleep in terms of relevant research studies. *(12 marks)*

hapter 3
hysiological psychology
Biological rhythms, sleep, dreams

Biological rhythms
Sleep   >
Dreams

Function of sleep: ecological (explanations)
Function of sleep: ecological (studies)
Function of sleep: restoration (explanations)
Function of sleep: restoration (studies)

In a nutshell – REM sleep is important for brain growth and repair whereas SWS is important for bodily restoration.

Research support
Case studies of total sleep deprivation (Peter Tripp, Randy Gardner) have provided evidence for the body's resilience to deprivation of sleep.

However ... these case studies have three main limitations: unique characteristics of the participants, contradictory findings and lack of scientific control.

Explanation 1: REM sleep and brain recovery (OSWALD, 1969)

Drug overdose
Patients recovering from drug overdoses and CNS injuries show significant increases in REM sleep during their recovery period.

Babies
Large amount of REM sleep in babies reflects rapid brain growth.

Replenishment of neurotransmitters
During REM sleep, neurons that have been active during the day cease firing but continue to synthesise new neurotransmitters for the next day.

However ... research has found little evidence that intense physical exercise does anything other than make people fall asleep faster.

A problem with this explanation is that ... REM sleep involves considerable neural activity, which uses up neurotransmitters. Their replenishment cannot, therefore, be the sole function of REM sleep.

A further problem for this explanation is that ... symptoms of severe depression are *reduced* in some people when deprived of REM sleep; also there is some contradictory evidence that complete REM deprivation has no significant ill effects.

Explanation 2: SWS and bodily restoration (OSWALD, 1969)

Hormonal activity
- The increase in the body's hormonal activities during SWS suggests a restoration process in the body.
- SWS is associated with the secretion of *growth hormones*, important for the synthesis of proteins, which need to be constantly restored.

Increase in NREM sleep after deprivation
Berger and Oswald (1962) found a marked increase in NREM on the first night after sleep deprivation while REM remained the same.

Supported by the finding that ... SWS deprivation in fibrositis sufferers leads to non-restorative sleep patterns.

However ... Horne (1988) highlighted the fact that amino acids are only freely available for 5 hours after a meal, making protein synthesis during SWS unlikely.

However ... some research has found no differences in the effects of partial sleep deprivation (REM or SWS) or total sleep deprivation (REM *and* SWS).

Explanation 3: Core sleep (HORNE, 1988)

Core sleep
Core sleep = REM + SWS, which is responsible for normal brain functioning (Horne, 1988).

Lighter stages of NREM
These are not essential and are therefore *optional sleep*.

Bodily restoration
This takes place during periods of relaxed wakefulness, while core sleep provides for restoration of brain systems.

This explanation is supported by ... Horne (1988), who reviewed 50 studies where people had been deprived of sleep – very few reported that this interfered with the ability to perform physical exercise.

Also ... runners slept for only an hour more after physical exertion (Shapiro et al., 1981).

The view that sleep is necessary for bodily restoration is challenged by ... the finding that participants given exhausting tasks went to sleep *faster* but not for *longer* (Horne and Minard, 1985).

Probable questions
1. Discuss **one or more** restoration theories of sleep. (24 marks)

Possible questions
2. (a) Describe the restoration account of sleep. (12 marks)

   (b) Evaluate the restoration account of sleep in terms of relevant research studies. (12 marks)

3. (a) Outline and evaluate **one** ecological account of the function of sleep. (12 marks)

   (b) Outline and evaluate **one** restoration account of the function of sleep. (12 marks)

Chapter 3	Biological rhythms	Function of sleep: ecological (explanations)
Physiological psychology	Sleep >	Function of sleep: ecological (studies)
Biological rhythms, sleep, dreams	Dreams	Function of sleep: restoration (explanations)
		Function of sleep: restoration (studies)

Sleep deprivation studies are used to test the assumption that sleep has an important restorative function.

Studies 1: Total sleep deprivation

- **Peter Tripp** After 3 days he became abusive; after 5 days he hallucinated and became paranoid; after 8 days his brain waves resembled those of a sleeping state. After 24 hours' sleep he recovered.
- **Randy Gardner** After 11 days no abnormal symptoms were present.

There are 3 main limitations of these case studies: the unique characteristics of the participants, contradictory findings and lack of scientific control.

However ... it is impossible to prevent microsleep in these studies, so participants may not be completely sleep-deprived.

In general ... case studies show no significant effects of sleep deprivation.

Studies 2: REM sleep deprivation

REM sleep deprivation increases the tendency to enter REM sleep earlier and increases the proportion of REM sleep on subsequent nights (REM rebound) (Empson, 2002).

However ... symptoms of severe depression are *reduced* in some people when deprived of REM sleep.

Some contradictory evidence ... exists that complete REM deprivation has no significant ill effects, e.g. one brain-injured patient who led a normal life without REM sleep (Lavie *et al.*, 1984).

Studies 3: SWS sleep deprivation

Moldofsky *et al.* (1975) found that:
- Fibrositis patients experience tiredness and EEG patterns in SWS are faster (therefore SWS is not restorative).
- Volunteers deprived of SWS sleep experienced symptoms of fibrositis.

However ... some research has found no differences in the effects of partial sleep deprivation (REM *or* SWS) or total sleep deprivation (REM *and* SWS).

Also ... SWS effects are unlikely – protein synthesis uses amino acids which are not available 5 hours after a meal (Horne, 1988).

Studies 4: Horne's explanation

- **Berger and Walker (1972)** found a large increase in SWS at the expense of the later stages on the first night after deprivation. There was an increase in REM on subsequent nights.
- **Sterne and Morgane (1974)** found no evidence of REM rebound following sleep deprivation for patients on antidepressants.

This supports the view that ... stage 4 and REM sleep constitute 'core' sleep, as participants were almost completely recovered following deprivation, and that lighter stages have no restorative function.

This can be explained because ... antidepressant drugs increase levels of available dopamine and serotonin, so there is no need for an REM rebound.

Probable questions

1. Discuss **two or more** research studies relating to the restoration account of sleep. *(24 marks)*
2. (a) Outline the restoration account of sleep. *(6 marks)*
   (b) Discuss research studies relating to the restoration account of sleep. *(18 marks)*

Possible questions

3. (a) Describe the restoration account of sleep. *(12 marks)*
   (b) Evaluate the restoration account of sleep in terms of relevant research studies. *(12 marks)*

Chapter 3
Physiological psychology
Biological rhythms, sleep, dreams >

Biological rhythms
Sleep
Dreams >

The nature of dreams
Neurobiological theories of dreaming
Psychological theories of dreaming

The content of dreams

The content of dreams varies hugely and is almost certainly unpredictable.

What do we dream about?
Dreams frequently have a noticeable emotional content which tends to be more negative than pleasurable; the dreamer often takes the role of an impartial observer (Hobson *et al.*, 2000).

Whom do we dream about?
The dreamer is almost always personally involved with the dream's characters. Kahn *et al.* (2000) found that half the characters in dreams were known to the dreamer, one-third were generic and less than 1 in 6 were unknown.

Who dreams about what?
• Males dream about other males more than females dream about males (Martin, 2000).
• People undergoing life crises have dreams reflecting this (Cartwright *et al.*, 1997).

Does the content mean anything?
• **Neurobiological theories** Dreams are meaningless, the result of random neurological activity during REM sleep, e.g. activation-synthesis.
• **Psychological theories** The content of dreams is highly relevant, e.g. Freud's theory: dreams permit unconscious fulfillment of wishes.

Cultural background influences the type of dream, e.g. people in hunter–gatherer societies dream more of animals than do US students (Domhoff, 2002).

The duration of dreams

• The duration of dreams is thought to correspond to the duration of REM sleep.
• Most dreams occur during REM sleep, which occurs every 90 minutes during sleep and lasts about 20 minutes.
• Dreams run 'in real time' and fade rapidly after waking.

Supported by ... research (e.g. Dement and Kleitman, 1957) that demonstrates the direct relationship between REM activity and the duration of a dream.

However ... it is impossible to measure the length of NREM dreams except by subjective report.

Different kinds of dream

Most dreaming occurs in REM sleep but we also dream, albeit differently, in NREM sleep.

REM dreams
Dement and Kleitman (1957) found that when sleepers were woken during REM sleep, they reported dreaming 80% of the time.

NREM dreams
These are shorter, more mundane and more fragmentary than REM dreams, and occur less often.

Hypnagogic dreams
These occur in the transitional state between wakefulness and sleep.

Hypnopompic states
These occur between sleep and wakefulness. Both hypnagogic and hypnopopic states are considered a 'reduced' version of normal dreaming.

Lucid dreams
Lucid dreamers report being fully aware of what they are dreaming, and can control events.

A problem is that ... only adults have been studied within a laboratory setting, so findings might not apply in other settings and other age groups.

Physiological evidence
The distinction between REM and NREM dreams is confirmed at neurobiological level (PET scans).

Distinction supported by ... Strauch and Meier (1996) who found little evidence of dreamers' emotional involvement in NREM dreams but plenty in REM dreams.

Objective evidence for lucid dreaming
LaBerge *et al.* (1981) found that lucid dreamers used eye movements to signal the beginning and end of dream intervals during REM sleep. These corresponded to actual elapsed time.

Probable questions
1. Discuss research related to the nature of dreams. (24 marks)

Possible questions
2. Discuss research related to **two** aspects of the nature of dreams (e.g. content, duration, relation with the stages of sleep). (24 marks)

Chapter 3
Physiological psychology
Biological rhythms, sleep, dreams >

Biological rhythms
Sleep
Dreams >

The nature of dreams
Neurobiological theories of dreaming
Psychological theories of dreaming

Theory 1: Activation-synthesis hypothesis

In a nutshell – There is random electrical activity during sleep: this is experienced as a dream. Dreams have no intrinsic meaning – meaningfulness is not what drives the dream.

Activation

- The brainstem generates spontaneous random signals during REM sleep.

- The body is paralysed so there is no other sensory input or motor output.

- For the cortex these signals are indistinguishable from the internal and external stimuli that are usually processed.

Synthesis

When activity arising from the brainstem is mixed with stored images from memory, the brain attempts to 'interpret' these, often resulting in bizarre images which we experience as dreams.

Supported by ... PET scans showing that the brainstem is active during REM sleep (supporting the *activity* part of the model), and that the prefrontal cortex is inactive during REM sleep (supporting the *synthesis* part of the model) (Braun *et al.*, 1997).

Challenging evidence

- Solms (2000) found that in patients with damage to the brainstem, REM activity ceased but dreaming continued, suggesting that REM activity and dreaming may be independent.

- Some studies have found that many dreams are coherent and consistent over time (Domhoff, 1996).

An alternative explanation is ... the AIM model (Hobson, 1992), which includes *activation* of the brain, external or internal *inputs* and *modulators*. Waking, REM and NREM states vary in levels of A, I and M.

Theory 2: Reverse learning

In a nutshell – The brain requires memory consolidation to use space more efficiently. Consolidation takes place during sleep, and the associated electrical activity is experienced as a dream.

Parasitic memories

Dreaming is a mechanism for 'unlearning' superfluous associations that arise from the vast amount of incoming information we store in memory.

Reverse learning

- This makes important memories more accessible, and makes storage in neural networks more compact, without the memory overlap caused by unwanted associations.

- This is adaptive because we can have smaller, more efficient brains.

Neurobiological mechanism

Random stimulation of the forebrain by the brainstem excites neurons corresponding to the unwanted associations. Their synapses are modified to make future activation less likely.

Research support

- Goertzel (1997) – even allowing for compression of information, the brain takes in far more than it can store.

- Mammals without REM sleep have a disproportionately large cortex to compensate for the extra storage capacity needed (Mukhametov, 1987).

Challenging evidence

- Brains of mammals that lack sleep have cortexes that are not as highly folded as human cortexes so may *not* have a much larger capacity.

- Christos (1996) found that computer simulations of reverse learning have shown that the number of parasitic memories is *increased* not decreased.

Main problem: no one neurobiological activity is equivalent to the state of dreaming.

Probable questions
1. Discuss **two or more** neurobiological theories of the functions of dreaming. *(24 marks)*

Possible questions
2. (a) Outline and evaluate research related to the nature of dreams. *(12 marks)*

(b) Outline and evaluate **one** neurobiological theory of the functions of dreaming. *(12 marks)*

hapter 3	Biological rhythms	The nature of dreams
hysiological psychology	Sleep	Neurobiological theories of dreaming
Biological rhythms, sleep, dreams >	Dreams >	**Psychological theories of dreaming**

Theory 1: Freud's psychoanalytic approach

In a nutshell – Dreams provide a 'royal road' to the unconscious mind.

Primary-process thought
Unacceptable id thoughts are repressed into the unconscious, but must be released through dreams.

Wish fulfilment
Dreams are the unconscious fulfilment of wishes that cannot be satisfied in the conscious mind.
Dream contents are expressed symbolically. The real meaning of a dream (the *latent content*) is transformed into a more innocuous form (the *manifest content*).

Physiological evidence
PET scans show that during REM sleep, the rational part of the brain (prefrontal cortex) is *inactive* whereas forebrain centres concerned with memory and motivation (irrational part) are *active*.

Cognitive evidence
Neural networks (Hopfield *et al.*, 1983) deal with overload by condensing 'memories', which supports Freud's view of dreaming as *condensation*.

Nightmares
Freud did not believe that all dreams constituted wish fulfilment: some (e.g. nightmares) fulfil other functions.

Problems with Freud's theory
- Claims for the purpose of dreams are difficult to falsify (a requirement of scientific theories).
- Freud's theory was based on his own experiences, and on case studies that consisted of a *historically* and *culturally biased* sample.

Theory 2: Jung's theory

In a nutshell – Dreams reflect not only the unconscious mind but also our current preoccupations.

Imbalance between the conscious and unconscious mind
This is dealt with by the process of *compensation* in dreams. Associations that arise when thinking about a dream can give clues to its meaning through the process of *amplification*.

Creative ideas
Creative ideas can come to us through dreams, e.g. Stevenson's idea for the plot of The Strange Case of Dr Jekyll and Mr Hyde.

Collective unconscious
Dreams may reveal the collective unconscious, expressing it using symbols that are common to all members of that culture.

There is some support for the claim because ... creativity in dreams can be seen among musicians and inventors.

Supported by ... Watson (2003), who found that personality characteristics were the most significant factor in dream recall – those high in imagination and fantasy were more likely to remember dreams and report them with vivid imagery.

Theory 3: Dreams as problem-solving (CARTWRIGHT, 1989)

In a nutshell – Dreams directly reflect our major conscious emotional concerns. Dreams serve an important mood regulation function.

Dreams as symbols
These symbols convey real concerns rather than disguising them.

Solving problems
- This includes problems *with* solutions (e.g. work problems) and problems *without* solutions (e.g. emotional problems).
- Research evidence: dream recall is increased at times of emotional stress.

The claim that problems appear in dreams is supported by the finding that ... people undergoing marital separation had dreams reflecting waking coping strategies (Cartwright *et al.*, 1997).

Dreams help to solve problems
Students reported dreams that reflected solutions to problems (Barrett, 1993).

However ... research with trauma survivors found very low rates of dream recall (Lavie and Kaminer, 1991).

Probable questions
1. Discuss **two or more** psychological theories of the functions of dreaming. *(24 marks)*
2. (a) Outline and evaluate **one** neurobiological theory of the functions of dreaming. *(12 marks)*
   (b) Outline and evaluate **one** psychological theory of the functions of dreaming. *(12 marks)*

Possible questions
3. (a) Outline and evaluate research related to the nature of dreams. *(12 marks)*
   (b) Outline and evaluate **one** psychological theory of the functions of dreaming. *(12 marks)*

Chapter 4

Cognitive psychology

Perceptual processes/development>

The visual system >

Perceptual organisation

Perceptual development

The structure and function of the visual system

The nature of visual information processing

The eye

The human eye has evolved to be sensitive to one particular form of electromagnetic energy – light.

Structure

Light enters through the pupil; the iris regulates the amount of light reaching inside the eye. The cornea and lens bend light rays and focus them onto the fovea, an area of the retina specialised for high visual acuity.

Functions

Accommodation: the lens changes its shape and thus brings objects from the external world into focus on the retina.

Why is the pupil small?
To avoid overstimulating photosensitive cells. The smaller the opening, the more light is focused.

But ... the pupil *also* dilates when a person feels aroused. This has been shown to make people appear more attractive to others (Hess, 1965).

However ... some animals have other areas that are photosensitive (e.g. the pineal gland is used for setting the biological clock in birds and lizards).

The retina

Light coming from the outside world strikes the retina, which contains photosensitive receptors.

Visual receptors

Structure

Rods are more plentiful than cones. They differ in terms of their light-absorbing pigment: rods contain rhodopsin; cones have one of three types of pigment.

Functions

Rods are more sensitive to dim light. Cones, particularly in the fovea, have greater sensitivity to detail (visual acuity).

Retinal neurons

Structure

Visual receptors send input to bipolar cells, which pass it on to ganglion cells before exiting the eye at the blind spot.

Functions

Cones have a one-to-one relationship with ganglion cells, whereas the ratio of rods to ganglion cells is much higher. Ganglion cells convert light impulses into electrical energy.

Although the eye is sensitive to light ... it is not a camera, and records only what is important.

Why did the retina evolve backwards?
Because it was an outgrowth of the brain rather than a development of light sensitive cells on the skin.

Visual pathways

Nerve impulses are transmitted from the retina along the visual pathways to the visual cortex.

Structure

- Each eye receives information from both left and right visual fields.

- Nerve fibres from the eye partially cross at the optic chiasm, then split and travel to the lateral geniculate nucleus (LGN) in the thalamus.

Function of visual cortex (in occipital lobe)

Information from both eyes is mixed and binocular vision is created. Information arrives in area V1 and is passed to V2 for further processing.

Supporting evidence comes from ... split-brain patients, who are unable to name an object presented only in the right visual field, thus demonstrating the existence of separate visual hemifields.

Visual signals are not just restricted to one *pathway*
Research has shown the existence of two visual pathways. After processing in V1, visual signals split into the ventral stream (dealing with object recognition) and the dorsal stream (dealing with spatial perception).

A consequence of ... the dysfunction of any part of the visual system is *blindness*.

- Blindness may result from massive damage to the visual cortex.

- Early blindness tends to compromise perceptual ability if sight is later restored.

Probable questions

1. Discuss the structure **and** functions of the visual system. *(24 marks)*

2. Discuss the functions of the visual system. *(24 marks)*

Possible questions

3. Discuss the structure and functions of the retina and visual pathways. *(24 marks)*

hapter 4 | The visual system | > | The structure and function of the visual system
ognitive psychology | Perceptual organisation | | The nature of visual information processing
Perceptual processes/development | Perceptual development

Sensory adaptation

Sensory adaptation occurs when photoreceptors in the eye change sensitivity to a visual stimulus, enabling the retina to cope with conditions of more or less light.

Dark adaptation
For the first 10 minutes, cones are more sensitive than rods. After 10 minutes, rods have increased their sensitivity to a point where they are now more sensitive than cones (the rod–cone break). Rods reach their maximum sensitivity after 30 minutes.

Light adaptation
Pupils become smaller (admitting less light).

- Sensitivity of cones to light decreases.
- Sensitivity of rods to light also decreases.
- The process takes only seconds.

A consequence of reduced acuity is that ... in the dark, we lose the ability to see colour (rods take over from cones) and fine detail (rods have lower visual acuity).

Increased sensitivity can be explained by ... the fact that when light is detected by a photoreceptor, its energy breaks down the visual pigment molecules into simpler molecules, which must recombine before the molecule can respond again (cone pigments take 6 minutes to rejoin; rods take 30 minutes).

Contrast-processing

This allows us to see an object and separate it from the background, and to detect differences in brightness between two adjoining areas.

Intracellular (lateral inhibition network)
- Each retinal cell is both *excited* (by the part of the image that falls on it) and *inhibited* (by neighbouring cells).
- Looking at a grid of white lines on a black background produces the Hermann illusion of grey spots in the white area between the vertical and horizontal lines.

Intracellular (receptive field)
When a stimulus is presented to the centre of a ganglion cell's receptive field, the cell is excited, but it is inhibited if the stimulus is presented in the surrounding area.

Supported by ... Hartline et al. (1956) who found evidence in the horseshoe crab that a receptor gave a greater response if stimulated on its own than if receptors on either side were also stimulated.

Why contrast processing?
It enables the visual system to be efficient under varying light conditions, and assists in detecting edges, making it easier to identify objects.

Colour-processing

This requires the ability to compare the responses of different kinds of cone.

Trichromatic theory
The theory proposes that there are three types of cone, each maximally sensitive to only one colour: red, green or blue. The brain synthesises information from these cones to produce other colours.

Opponent-processing theory
Hering (1878) believed there were three opponent systems (blue–yellow, red–green and black–white). Activation of one member of the pair inhibits activity in the other.

Evidence for trichromatic theory
Dartnell et al. (1983) found:
- Red cones (most sensitive to long wavelengths)
- Green cones (most sensitive to medium wavelengths)
- Blue cones (most sensitive to short wavelengths).

Evidence for opponent-processing theory
DeValois (1960) found cells in the retina and LGN that responded to one wavelength with excitation and to another with inhibition.

Combining the theories
Rather than being seen as competing, these theories reflect physiological activity at a different stage of the visual system.

Probable questions

1. Describe and evaluate research (theories **and/or** studies) into **two** forms of visual information processing. *(24 marks)*
2. Discuss the nature of visual information processing. *(24 marks)*

Possible questions

3. (a) Outline the structure of the eye. *(6 marks)*

   (b) Discuss research (theories **and/or** studies) into **one** form of visual information processing. *(12 marks)*

Chapter 4	The visual system	Theories of visual perception: constructivist theories
Cognitive psychology	Perceptual organisation >	Theories of visual perception: direct theories
Perceptual processes/development>	Perceptual development	Explanations of perceptual organisation

Theory 1: Gregory (1972)

In a nutshell – Perceptions are constructions 'from floating fragmentary scraps of data, signalled by the senses and drawn from the brain's memory banks' (Gregory, 1974).

Perception as hypothesis testing
The brain makes use of stored knowledge to make sense of sensory data received through the eyes.

Expectations
Expectations may be generated by the context in which an object is viewed (e.g. Palmer, 1975).

Perceptual 'guesswork' and illusions
• **Non-sensed object characteristics** We respond to some objects even though we don't have all the sensory data necessary.

• **Ambiguous perceptions** Figures such as the Necker cube provide no clues as to which of two alternative hypotheses is correct, so the perceptual system switches between the two.

• **Likely and unlikely objects** Our knowledge of objects with which we are familiar may cause us to misperceive objects that are less likely.

Strengths
The theory can explain how our perceptual system deals with ambiguous figures or a poor retinal image, and why it is difficult to train computers to 'perceive'.

Limitations
It suggests that perception is often *inaccurate*. It fails to explain perception in infants, who have no prior perceptual experience.

Supported by ... studies of perceptual set (e.g. Bruner and Minturn, 1955) which demonstrate the influence of expectations in perception.

Supported by ... the role of 'guesswork' – illusions can be explained as 'misapplied hypotheses' that *normally* work in the real world, e.g. the Müller–Lyer illusion.

Cross-cultural research supports the view that ... perception is a 'construction', e.g. the finding that people who do not live in 'carpentered' environments are not as susceptible to the Müller–Lyer illusion.

However ... the 'misapplied hypothesis' explanation of Müller–Lyer illusion is not supported by the fact that if fins are replaced by circles the illusion persists, and there was no effect when a participant walked around a 3D model (Wraga et al., 2000).

Theory 2: Gestalt approach

In a nutshell – Cues from perceptual data elicit higher-level responses, the combination of which leads to perception.

Laws of perceptual organisation
These include the laws of *proximity* (elements that are physically closer together are grouped together perceptually) and *closure* (figures are 'completed' even when part of the information is missing).

Figure and background
We have a tendency to see objects (figures) and surfaces (background) rather than simply sensations of light.

Strengths
Gestalt approach has had an enduring influence on psychology because of its holist approach to perceptual experience.

Limitations
The approach explains how we organise *proximal* stimuli, but not how we organise *distal* stimuli.

Research support
• Navon (1977) demonstrated that the 'whole does not equal the sum of its parts' (people identify a large letter made up of lots of smaller ones more easily than the small letters).

• Zapadia et al. (1995) demonstrated neurological support for the law of similarity (the visual cortex contains neurons which respond to a line of a certain orientation).

Probable questions
1. Describe and evaluate **one** constructivist theory of visual perception. *(24 marks)*
2. Describe and evaluate **one or more** constructivist theories of visual perception. *(24 marks)*

Possible questions
3. Outline and evaluate **two** constructivist theories of visual perception. *(24 marks)*
4. (a) Outline and evaluate **one** constructivist theory of visual perception. *(12 marks)*
   (b) Outline and evaluate **one** direct theory of visual perception. *(12 marks)*

Chapter 3	The visual system	Theories of visual perception: constructivist theories
Physiological psychology	Perceptual organisation >	Theories of visual perception: direct theories
Perceptual processes/development>	Perceptual development	Explanations of perceptual organisation

Theory 1: Gibson's ecological theory (1979)

In a nutshell – The raw material of the senses is sufficient for us to make visual sense of the world around us (a 'bottom-up' approach).

Optic array
The pattern of light reaching the eye provides us with information about the layout of objects in space.
- **Optic flow** As the observer moves, each light ray moves producing a transformation of the optic array.
- **Ecological aspects** Objects have texture, changing with distance from an object.
- **Invariant features** of the environment (such as texture density and size constancy) supply information crucial for accurate perception.

Affordances
Many objects have directly perceivable properties that offer (or afford) opportunities for action.
- **Role of experience** Direct perception depends on our ability to pick up information that specifies the affordance, which depends on our experiences.

Supported by ... research performed with trainee pilots which showed that all the perceptual information required lay in the optic array (Gibson et al., 1955).

Research support: biological motion
Johansson (1973) found that we perceive motion simply from a changing array of dots, thus demonstrating an innate ability to recover movement information from sparse visual input.

Research support: 'time to contact'
Judging distance and speed with respect to time using only visual (direct) information – research with gannets (Lee, 1980) and long-jumpers (Lee et al., 1982) suggests this is an innate ability.

Strengths
- The theory provides an account of perception appropriate for animals, babies and adults.
- Gibson's explanations of illusions tend to be more successful than Gregory's.

Limitations
The theory cannot adequately explain how perception is influenced by situation and culture.

Theory 2: Marr's computational model (1982)

In a nutshell – The goal of any visual system is to produce representations of the environment, and the goal of perception is to make computations that make sense of these computations.

Primal sketch
Records variations in light intensity across the retina, allowing the detection of surfaces and boundaries.

2½D sketch
Information about depth of each point is used to discover properties of surfaces.

3D model
A perceptual representation is transformed into one appropriate for recognition.

Supported by ... Benson and Greenberg (1969), whose patient S had the ability to make a primal sketch but no more.

Strengths
Unlike other theories, Marr's account suggests how the visual system might actually *work*.

Limitations
- Full details of the system were yet to be completed when Marr died at a young age.
- The system cannot cope with situations of ambiguity without extra information.

Top-down and bottom-up
- Neisser (1976) proposed a model that involves bottom-up *and* top-down processes, but this would be slow and thus unlikely.
- Each may be appropriate in different circumstances – bottom-up when optic array is rich and top-down when it is poor.
- Norman (2001) suggests that *object recognition* may involve top-down processes, and *spatial perception* bottom-up processes.

Probable questions
1. Describe and evaluate **one** direct theory of visual perception.		*(24 marks)*
2. Describe and evaluate **one or more** direct theories of visual perception.		*(24 marks)*

Possible questions
3. Outline and evaluate **two** direct theories of perception.		*(24 marks)*
4. Describe and evaluate **one or more** theories of visual perception.		*(24 marks)*

Chapter 4

Cognitive psychology

Perceptual processes/development>

The visual system

Perceptual organisation   >

Perceptual development

Theories of visual perception: constructivist theories

Theories of visual perception: direct theories

Explanations of perceptual organisation

Explanation 1: Depth (distance)

Binocular cues (relying on data from both eyes) and monocular cues (requiring data from only one eye) are used by the brain to judge depth (or distance).

Monocular depth cues
These include relative size, texture gradient, interposition, linear perspective and motion parallax.

Binocular depth cues
These include *binocular convergence* (muscle tension associated with looking at close objects provides information about distance) and *retinal disparity* (closer objects provide more disparate images in the two eyes).

Research support from ... the distorted Ames room, which plays on our use of relative size as a depth cue, causing familiar objects to appear to be different sizes.

Constructivist explanations are challenged by ... the finding that a figure's relative height to the apparent horizon is more important (Seckel and Klarke, 1997). Gibson identified this horizon-ratio relation as an invariant aspect of the optic array.

Explanation 2: Movement

The perception of movement includes the perception of real movement as well as the perception of apparent movement.

Apparent movement
Objects appear to move in the *phi phenomenon* (alternate lights go on and off in succession), and in *induced movement* (a framed object appears to move against its background).

Real movement
Cues include movement across the retina (interpreted as movement of the object), movement of the eyes and movement of the head (interpreted as following the progress of a moving object).

Research support from ... Ames (1949) who showed that the inflation of an illuminated balloon in a darkened room was interpreted as the balloon moving closer to the observer.

Direct or constructivist?
A direct explanation would predict perception of changing size (no observer movement) whereas the constructivist explanation is that our visual system *prefers* the 'moving closer' hypothesis as it is a more common experience.

Research in this area has been applied to ... motion pictures, neon lights and traffic 'rumble lines'.

Explanation 3: Constancies

Our tendency is to see the properties of objects as being invariant despite any changes in the retinal stimulus.

Size constancy
Familiar objects are perceived as the same size despite changes in size of retinal image, indicating a change in distance.

Shape constancy
Knowledge of familiar objects means we see their shape as unchanging despite changes in viewing angle.

Colour constancy
Most colour surfaces appear the same when viewed under different lighting conditions.

Research support: the Ponzo illusion ... causes the observer to perceive lines of the same length as different.

Constructivist or direct?
Stimulus-relation theory explains that the context in which a stimulus appears affects how it is perceived. When context information is unavailable, viewers use prior knowledge to judge an object's size.

Research support: the trapezium illusion ... causes us to assume that the object is familiar and moving in a predictable way.

This can be explained by ... retinex theory (Land, 1977). Although the absolute wavelengths of colours change in dim light, relative wavelengths do not.

Probable questions

1. Outline and evaluate **two or more** explanations of perceptual organisation. (24 marks)

2. Critically consider explanations of **two or more** types of perceptual organisation (e.g. depth, movement, constancies, illusions). (24 marks)

Possible questions

3. Outline and evaluate **one or more** explanations of perceptual organisation. (24 marks)

Chapter 4 | The visual system | **Development of perceptual abilities (studies)**
Cognitive psychology | Perceptual organisation | Explanations of perceptual development
Perceptual processes/development> | Perceptual development > | The nature–nurture debate in perception

Development of depth (distance) perception

Infant studies
Children who have not had visual experience can be used to see if a perceptual skill is innate or learned.

- **Yonas et al. (2001)** The ability to use shadows as a cue to depth develops with age.
- **Gibson and Walk (1960)** Six-month-olds appeared to use depth cues, refusing to crawl over the 'deep' side of the visual cliff.

Cross-cultural studies
People from different cultures have different experiences: these are compared to test the effect of experience.

- **Turnbull (1963)** People who lived in dense forest lacked ability to use relative size as a distance cue.
- **Hudson (1960)** Bantu children lacked the ability to use monocular depth cues compared with European children.

This finding is consistent with other evidence ... e.g. Yonas *et al.* (1986), who found that responsiveness to depth cues develops at about 6 months.

However ... infants may have had sufficient experience to have learned depth cues. Other research with younger infants (e.g. Scarr and Salapek, 1970) found no wariness – though wariness may develop later.

Two conclusions that can be drawn from these findings
- Formal schooling didn't influence the children's perceptual skills.
- Monocular depth cues are learned rather than innate.

Development of visual constancies

Infant studies
- **Bower (1966)** Infants aged 2 months displayed shape constancy, i.e. responded to an objective shape rather than the retinal image of an object.
- **Slater et al. (1990)** Infants showed size constancy, i.e. differentiated between cubes at different distances despite fact they looked the same size.

Cross-cultural studies
- **Allport and Pettigrew (1957)** Rural Zulus displayed less shape constancy than urban Zulus.
- **Segall et al. (1963)** Zulus who didn't live in a 'carpentered' environment were less susceptible to the Müller–Lyer illusion, i.e. they displayed less size constancy.

Research support: shape constancy
Slater and Morrison (1985) found that newborns also display shape constancy.

This suggests that ... this is an innate ability.

Research support
Evidence on size constancy is support for Gibson's (1979) view of direct perception.

In contrast to infant studies ... cross-cultural studies suggest some aspects of constancies are learned.

But this may be due to ... researcher and/or participant effects.

Limitations of infant studies
- Abilities present at birth are not necessarily innate and abilities that appear later in development are not necessarily learned.
- Assessment of infant abilities is hampered by a lack of development of motor skills and acuity.

Limitations of cross-cultural studies
- We cannot be sure that participants and researchers have fully understood each other.
- These were natural experiments so we can't assume that the IV has caused differences in perceptual abilities.

Probable questions
1. Describe and evaluate studies of the development of perceptual abilities. *(24 marks)*
2. (a) Outline and evaluate **one or more** infant studies of the development of perceptual abilities. *(12 marks)*
   (b) Outline and evaluate **one or more** cross-cultural studies of the development of perceptual abilities. *(12 marks)*

Possible questions
3. Outline and evaluate either infant or cross-cultural studies of the development of perceptual abilities. *(24 marks)*

Chapter 4
Cognitive psychology
Perceptual processes/development>

The visual system
Perceptual organisation
Perceptual development   >

Development of perceptual abilities (studies)
Explanations of perceptual development
The nature–nurture debate in perception

Nativist explanations

In a nutshell – These are bottom-up, *nativist* views that perceptual development arises from innate ways of organising sensory experience.

Theory of direct perception (Gibson)
This theory suggests that perception is largely innate.

- **Optic array** The pattern of light reaching the eye provides us with information about the layout of objects in space.

- **Affordances** Many objects have directly perceivable properties that offer (or afford) opportunities for action.

Differentiation theory (Gibson and Gibson, 1955)
- Perceptual development is a process of learning to see the differences between objects.
- Experience leads us to identify properties that make 2 objects different.
- Infants are amodal, i.e. born with little differentiation between the different sensory modalities (vision, hearing and so on).

This explanation is supported by ... studies of biological motion and innate depth perception (Gibson and Walk's study of the visual cliff).

However infant studies have limitations ... e.g. research shows evidence of some perceptual learning in the womb.

Challenged by studies that show the influence of expectations, e.g. Bruner and Minturn (1955) found that 13 was perceived as a letter/number depending on expectations.

Supported by ... infant studies which suggest that many perceptual abilities are innate, e.g. Bower (1966) found that infants had shape constancy while Fantz (1961) showed that face preference is innate.

However ... some cross-cultural research suggests that aspects of depth perception are learned, e.g. Hudson (1960) found cultural/learned differences in the interpretation of monocular cues for depth perception.

Challenged by ... research that suggests infants are not amodal, e.g. infants were distressed when they saw their mothers in one place but heard their voices coming from somewhere else (Aronson and Rosenbloom, 1971).

Constructivist explanations

In a nutshell – These are top-down, *empiricist* views that we learn to perceive the world through our experiences of it.

Constructivist theory (Gregory)
Three-dimensional perception is *constructed* and related to cultural differences.

- **Hypothesis testing** The brain makes use of stored knowledge to interpret sensory data.

- **Non-sensed object characteristics** We respond to some objects even though we don't have all the sensory data necessary.

Enrichment theory (Piaget, 1954)
- Sensory data are often impoverished and ambiguous.
- They are 'enriched' by cognitive schemas (expectations).
- Infants develop schemas through experience.
- We gradually build more complex schemas to enable the development of full perceptual abilities.

Constructivist theory is supported by studies on expectations, e.g. Palmer (1975) who found that a mailbox was 'seen' as a loaf in a kitchen setting **which shows that ...** expectations influence perception.

Challenged by ... situations where perception is highly accurate; constructivist theory suggests that it is often inaccurate.

Supported by ... Yonas et al. (2001) who found the use of shadows for depth perception develops with age.

However ... Held and Hein (1963), using the kitten carousel, showed that perceptual experience on its own is not enough. Sensory and motor experiences are necessary.

However ... both constructivist and enrichment theories relate to impoverished input – some sensory data are complete and do not need expectations.

Probable questions

1. Outline and evaluate **two or more** explanations of perceptual development.   *(24 marks)*

Possible questions

2. (a) Discuss **one or more** explanations of the development of perceptual abilities.   *(12 marks)*

   (b) To what extent do these explanations contribute to the nature–nurture debate in perception?   *(12 marks)*

Chapter 4 | The visual system | Development of perceptual abilities (studies)
Cognitive psychology | | Explanations of perceptual development
Perceptual processes/development> | Perceptual organisation |
Perceptual development > | The nature–nurture debate in perception

Nature

In a nutshell – The nativist view is that perceptual development arises from innate ways of organising sensory experience.

Theory of direct perception (Gibson)
This suggests that perception is largely innate (evidence for the 'nature' position).

Infant studies
Infant studies have looked at depth perception and visual constancies; also Fantz (1961) showed that babies have an innate preference for faces over random arrangements of the same features.

Studies of young animals
Gibson and Walk (1960) showed that the use of binocular cues for depth perception was innate, but monocular cues were not.

Studies of adults
Rosch (1978) suggests that the perception of colour is universal and not determined by cultural experiences.

Theory of direct perception is supported by ... studies of biological motion (e.g. Lee *et al.*) and innate depth perception (Gibson and Walk's study of the visual cliff).

However, this view is challenged by ... studies that show influence of expectations, e.g. Bruner and Minturn (1955) found that 13 was perceived as a letter/number depending on expectations.

There are possible confounding variables in this research ... e.g. further research (Fantz and Miranda, 1975) found that babies prefer patterns with rounded edges.

Although we cannot generalise from ... studies of animals to human behaviour, the fact that very young animals display depth perception makes evolutionary sense in that it ensures their survival.

Nurture

In a nutshell – The empiricist view is that we learn to perceive the world through our experiences of it.

Constructivist theory (Gregory)
Three-dimensional perception is constructed and related to cultural differences.

Cross-cultural studies
These tend to show that experience affects perceptual ability and so support the view that perception is related to experience.

Restricted experience
Blakemore and Cooper (1970) found that kittens raised without experience of a particular orientation of line later failed to respond to that orientation.

Perceptual deprivation
The study of SB (Gregory and Wallace, 1963) provides evidence for the effect of experience on the development of perception.

Constructivist theory is supported by ... studies on expectations, e.g. Palmer (1975) who found that a mailbox was 'seen' as a loaf in kitchen setting ***which shows that ...*** expectations influence perception.

However, this view is challenged by ... situations where perception is highly accurate; constructivist theory suggests that it is often inaccurate.

The influence of restricted experience on perception is confirmed in ... research that tested the activity of cells in the visual cortex (Hubel and Wiesel, 1970) and suggested a *critical period* for perceptual development.

The case study of SB is supported by ... similar studies of patients recovering from cataracts (e.g. von Senden, 1932).

Nature and nurture
The development of the brain (an innate system) relies on experience to direct it: therefore nature is meaningless without nurture, and vice versa.

Probable questions
1. Discuss the nature–nurture debate in perception. *(24 marks)*

Possible questions
2. (a) Outline **two or more** studies of the development of perceptual abilities. *(12 marks)*

(b) To what extent do these studies contribute to the nature–nurture debate in perception? *(12 marks)*

Chapter 5
Developmental psychology
Cognitive development >

Development of thinking >
Development of intelligence
Development of morality

Piaget's theory of cognitive development
Vygotsky's theory of cognitive development
Applications of theories of cognitive development

The mechanisms of cognitive development

These are the *causes* of developmental change. Piaget applied biological principles to the study of human development.

Schema
A schema is a self-constructed mental structure which develops from interaction with the environment.

Assimilation
Children try to understand new information in terms of existing knowledge.

Accommodation
This occurs when a child adapts an existing schema to cope with new information that does not appear to fit.

Equilibration
There is an imbalance between what is understood and what is encountered; the resulting disequilibrium leads to new schemas or the adaptation of existing ones.

Despite many criticisms ... Piaget has been enormously influential in education and in research into cognitive development.

The theory is culturally biased because ... it is based on studies of European children. In other cultures, concrete reasoning may be more highly regarded.

In addition ... the Vygotskian approach may be more appropriate for collectivist societies.

Piaget underestimated ... the effects of other factors on development (e.g. social and motivational influences).

There is little evidence to support the claim that ... cognitive development is driven by the need for equilibrium in cognitive structures.

Stages in cognitive development

Cognitive development proceeds through a series of four stages, each one qualitatively more advanced than the one preceding it.

Stage 1: Sensori-motor
This stage sees the co-ordination of sensory input with motor actions; a key development is *object permanence*.

Stage 2: Pre-operational
Thought becomes increasingly symbolic; children are incapable of *reversibility* and display *egocentrism* and *centration*.

Stage 3: Concrete operations
The rudiments of logical reasoning are developed, and the child now displays *reversibility* and *decentration*; a key development is *conservation*.

Stage 4: Formal operations
The child can now demonstrate *abstract skills*, *hypothetical-deductive reasoning* and *idealistic thinking*.

Limitations: object permanence (OP)
Piaget did not design his experiments carefully enough to exclude alternate explanations of OP (e.g. the child may know a missing object still exists but not how to uncover it). Bower et al. (1971) found evidence of OP at 4 months.

Methodological problems
Tasks were confusing, e.g. conservation failures may have been due to the use of 2 questions: when only 1 question was asked younger children were able to conserve (Samuel and Bryant, 1984).

Children may have been influenced by demand characteristics ... e.g. children may have been misled by deliberate transformation in the conservation study – this effect was overcome when 'naughty teddy' was used (McGarrigle and Donaldson, 1974).

The tasks were not meaningful ... e.g. the egocentrism task was easier using the policeman and naughty boy task than the 3 mountains task (Hughes, 1975).

Stage theories have been criticised ... for being too rigid; Piaget introduced the idea of *décalage* to cope with such criticisms.

Stages of development are representative mainly of Western society ... where formal operational thinking is highly prized. In non-Western cultures however, there may be a higher regard for the more basic level of concrete operations.

Probable questions
1. Describe and evaluate Piaget's theory of cognitive development. *(24 marks)*
2. Outline and evaluate **two** theories of cognitive development. *(24 marks)*

Possible questions
3. (a) Describe Piaget's theory of cognitive development. *(12 marks)*
   (b) To what extent can theories such as Piaget's be successfully applied (e.g. to education)? *(12 marks)*

Chapter 5	Development of thinking	>	Piaget's theory of cognitive development
Developmental psychology	Development of intelligence		**Vygotsky's theory of cognitive development**
Cognitive development	>	Development of morality		Applications of theories of cognitive development

Social nature of thought

Development occurs when children internalise the cultural tools of thinking learned through social interactions with more knowledgeable others.

Role of culture
Culture is the prime determinant of individual development.
- Children are born with *elementary* mental functions that are transformed into *higher* mental functions by the influence of culture.
- The 'expert' interacting with the child initially assumes most of the responsibility for guiding problem-solving, but this gradually transfers to the child (*scaffolding*).

Role of language
- Language initially takes the form of shared dialogues between adult and child; then the child uses inner dialogues as a way of solving problems.
- Every function appears twice: first, on the *social* level (between people), and later on the *individual* level (inside the child).

Zone of proximal development (ZPD)
The ZPD is the difference between an individual's current level of development and his/her potential level. The learner moves through the ZPD with the assistance of experts.

Strengths
- The approach is more positive than Piaget's as it offers ways in which others can actively assist a learner.
- It has potentially more educational applications (e.g. collaborative learning, scaffolding).

Limitations
It may 'overplay' the importance of social factors; if social influence were all that were needed, development would be faster.

Research support
- Effects of culture on cognitive development have been shown in cross-cultural research, e.g. the primitive counting system used in Papua New Guinea (Gredler, 1992).
- Nigerian children with no formal instruction in mathematics still developed specific mathematical skills as a result of their street trading transactions (Oloko, 1993).

However ... research suggests that social interaction does not always enhance learning, but can also impair it (e.g. Piaget's views).

Research support
The idea that language and thought are at first independent but later become interdependent is supported by Carmichael *et al.* (1932), who showed that labels affect how we remember things.

The role of the ZPD is supported by ... McNaughton and Leyland (1990), who observed young children working with their mothers on jigsaws of increasing difficulty. The greatest teaching input was at the edges of the ZPD.

Research studies

Scaffolding
Wood *et al.* (1976) found that some mothers gave *general* encouragement while others gave *specific* help.

Scientific and everyday concepts
Scientific concepts are better understood because they are learned through cultural interaction, whereas everyday concepts are learned through self-directed activity – a claim supported by Shif (1935).

The problem with scaffolding is that ... success depends on the tutor being sufficiently sensitive to the learner's needs.

Differences between Vygotsky and Piaget's theory may represent different kinds of learning and different kinds of learner (introvert and extrovert).

Probable questions
1. Describe and evaluate Vygotsky's theory of cognitive development. *(24 marks)*
2. (a) Outline **one** theory of cognitive development. *(6 marks)*
   (b) Outline and evaluate applications of theories of cognitive development (e.g. to education). *(18 marks)*

Possible questions
3. Compare and contrast Piaget's and Vygotsky's theories of cognitive development. *(24 marks)*

Chapter 5
Developmental psychology
Cognitive development >

Development of thinking >
Development of intelligence
Development of morality

Piaget's theory of cognitive development
Vygotsky's theory of cognitive development
Applications of theories of cognitive development

Application 1: Piaget's theory

Children develop intellectual autonomy rather than being 'empty vessels waiting to be filled with facts'.

Readiness
- Children are unable to acquire specific cognitive abilities until maturation gives them the necessary prerequisites.
- Specific educational recommendations could be made appropriate to the stage of a child's development.

Discovery learning
Piaget's theory assumes that education is a process of learning and not just the acquisition of a set of facts. True understanding can come only from active discovery.

Motivation
The teacher creates curiosity by providing the setting and appropriate materials.

However ... Bryant and Trabasso (1971) found that pre-operational children could be *trained* to solve transitive inference tasks.

In contrast ... Danner and Day (1977) found that tutoring on formal operational tasks had no effect.

The Plowden Report (1967) used Piaget's theory to recommend a *child-centred* approach in primary education, although this may have been little more than a theoretical justification for these changes (Walkerdine, 1984).

Limitations
- Criticisms of the theory undermine the validity of its educational application (Sylva, 1987).
- Discovery activities may be at the expense of content knowledge.
- The Piagetian view may be culture-biased as it concentrates on skills important in Western cultures.

Problems assessing teaching methods
- It is difficult to assess *real* learning as it is so complex.
- Teachers may use the same method, but the *practice* of this method may differ.

Application 2: Vygotsky's theory

Teachers and learners should collaborate with each other to create meaning in ways that children can then make their own.

Collaborative learning
Students at various performance levels work together towards a common goal.

Peer tutoring
Peers act as experts.

Zone of proximal development
When learners are in the ZPD for a particular task, providing scaffolding will enable them to achieve that task.

More knowledgeable other
The ZPD encompasses tasks that learners cannot perform on their own but can complete with help of a more knowledgeable other (MKO).

Scaffolding
MKOs provide support so that learners can accomplish tasks they could otherwise not complete.

Supported by ... Gokhale (1995), who found that students using collaborative learning performed better on a critical thinking test.

Supported by ... studies (e.g. Cohen *et al.*, 1982) that have shown that peer tutoring leads to an improvement in tutee's and tutor's academic and social development.

Limitations
- It may be more appropriate in collectivist settings (emphasis on interdependence among learners).
- It relies on the skills of peers and teachers.

Differences and similarities
- An ilnnate, individual process (Piaget) contradicts with a socially constructed, collaborative one (Vygotsky).
- Both theorists emphasise construction of knowledge and the active role of the learner.
- CASE approach *combines* the two approaches.

Overall *formal, teacher-oriented* approaches produce better performance in reading, maths and English but some teachers using *child-centred methods* produce the best results of all (Bennett, 1976). It may not be the method but the *application* of it that is crucial.

Probable questions
1. Discuss applications of **two or more** theories of cognitive development (e.g. to education). *(24 marks)*
2. Discuss applications of **one** theory of cognitive development. *(24 marks)*

Possible questions
3. (a) Outline **two** theories of cognitive development. *(12 marks)*
   (b) To what extent have these theories been successfully applied (e.g. to education)? *(12 marks)*

Chapter 5

Developmental psychology

Cognitive development   >

Development of thinking

Development of intelligence   >

Development of morality

The role of genetics in intelligence

Environmental factors in intelligence

Twin studies

Identical twins share 100% of their genes, whereas non-identical twins share 50%. If heredity affects intelligence then identical twins should be more similar because they share more genes.

Bouchard and McGue (1981)
The study found that even when identical twins are raised apart, their IQs correlate quite highly. This suggests that genetic contributions to intelligence are stronger than environmental influences.

Burt (1955)
Burt studied identical twins raised apart, concluding that genetic factors are more important than environmental factors in determining intelligence.

Limitations of twin studies
• They are natural experiments and therefore don't demonstrate a *causal* relationship.

• Later research has identified different degrees of 'identicalness'; for instance some twins share a different 'environment' in the womb.

However ... even when individuals share identical genes, their intelligence is not identical, so other (environmental) factors must be contributing.

A problem for Burt's claim is that ... Kamin (1974) accused him of inventing data. Although this accusation was challenged by Joynson (1989), the general view is that Burt was dishonest in his research.

Adoption studies

Adoption studies examine the resemblance between adopted children and their biological and adoptive parents.

Colorado Adoption Project (CAP)
Adopted children become increasingly like their biological parents and less like their adoptive parents as they get older (Plomin et al., 1997).

Conclusions that can be drawn from the CAP
• Heritable factors affect verbal intelligence more than other types of abilities.

• The influence of genetic factors becomes more apparent with age.

Other research

This includes investigations into controversial areas such as the high intelligence gene and race differences in IQ.

High intelligence gene
The *high intelligence gene* (IGF2R) was found twice as often in children with ultra-high IQs than in children with average IQs (Chorney et al., 1998).

Indirect genetic influences
• Genes cause a reaction in others that affects our development (reactive).

• Parents' genes determine aspects of their behaviour, e.g. producing an intellectually stimulating environment (passive).

Race and intelligence
Jensen (1969) found that racial differences between black and white Americans were due to genetic differences.

A problem in this research was that ... no common genetic factor was found in *all* those with high intelligence.

Research support for indirect genetic influences
Braungart et al. (1992) found a higher correlation for HOME scores and IQ among children brought up by their biological parents than among children brought up by adoptive parents.

Problems for Jensen's race and intelligence claim
• IQ tests may be *culturally biased*.

• Lower test scores may be due to lower motivation in some ethnic groups, or a self-fulfilling stereotype.

Probable questions

1. Discuss research (theories **and/or** studies) into the role of genetics in the development of measured intelligence. *(24 marks)*

2. Discuss research (theories **and/or** studies) into the development of measured intelligence. *(24 marks)*

Possible questions

3. (a) Outline and evaluate research (theories **and/or** studies) into the role of genetics in the development of measured intelligence. *(12 marks)*

   (b) Outline and evaluate research (theories **and/or** studies) into the role of environmental factors in the development of measured intelligence. *(12 marks)*

Chapter 5
Developmental psychology
Cognitive development   >

Development of thinking
Development of intelligence   >
Development of morality

The role of genetics in intelligence
Environmental factiors in intelligence

Factor 1: Intervention studies

Intervention studies were designed to boost scholastic achievement in children otherwise compromised by low IQ.

Mother love and IQ
Skeels and Dye (1939) found that children who received the individual attention of a mother substitute increased their IQ levels compared with controls; the differences persisted into adulthood.

Perry pre-school project
This involved at-risk children, aged 3–4, given a high quality pre-school programme. This had a positive effect on IQ, achievement, long-term earnings and crime rates.

Attachment may boost IQ because ...
- attachment provides children with a secure base to explore (and learn)
- lack of attachment leads to excess of stress hormones, which slow mental growth (Carlson et al., 1995).

Findings supported by other studies ... e.g. Project Headstart in the 1960s, which also found long-term beneficial effects.

Factor 2: Living conditions

Certain features of a child's home culture affect intellectual development.

Home environment
The most significant positive influences were parental involvement, provision of age-appropriate play materials and opportunities for daily stimulation (Bradley et al., 1988).

The Flynn effect (1996)
Since 1940, children's IQ scores have been increasing by about 3 points per decade. This can be explained in terms of improved environmental influences.

Findings consistent with the theories of ... Piaget and Vygotsky, although each would emphasise different aspects of such interactions.

However ... improvement may be due to the fact that people have got better at doing IQ tests over time.

Factor 3: Diet

There is increasing evidence that dietary interventions can affect IQ.

Vitamin–mineral supplements
Poorly nourished children who received vitamin–mineral supplements performed better in non-verbal IQ than a placebo group (Schoenthaier and Bier, 1999).

Brain chemicals
Concentrations of NAA and choline alter with brain disease or injury. High levels of NAA and low levels of choline are associated with high IQ (Jung et al., 1999).

This shows that ... children who are 'adequately nourished' tend to come from homes that are also stimulating, and therefore may already be nearer the top of their reaction range.

Factor 4: Race

Psychologists have studied children adopted transracially.

The Minnesota study
Scarr and Weinberg (1983) studied black and interracial children adopted by white parents. At age 7, these children had higher IQ scores than average for respective groups.

However ... a follow-up study at age 17 found adoption had produced little lasting increase in the IQ of the black children.

This suggests that ... IQ is determined by complex genetic mechanisms which have little to do with race.

Nature and nurture: phenylketonuria
PKU is an inherited condition that can lead to mental retardation.

However ... a diet low in phenylalanine (environment) means that this genetic condition is not expressed.

Probable questions
1. Discuss research (theories **and/or** studies) into the role of environmental factors in the development of measured intelligence. (24 marks)
2. Critically consider the role of genetics **and** environmental factors in the development of measured intelligence. (24 marks)

Possible questions
3. Describe and evaluate research into **two or more** environmental factors associated with the development of measured intelligence. (24 marks)

Chapter 5	Development of thinking	**Theories of moral understanding development**
Developmental psychology	Development of intelligence	Gender and cultural differences
Cognitive development >	Development of morality >	

Theory 1: Kohlberg's (1969) theory

In a nutshell – Moral reasoning is the basis for moral behaviour. People progress through six stages which can be more generally classified into three levels.

Main features
- The stages are invariant and universal.
- Each stage represents a more equilibriated form of moral understanding.
- Each stage is an organised whole.
- Moral maturity is achieved through maturation, disequilibrium and gains in perspective taking.

Stages
- **Pre-conventional level (stages 1 and 2)** Children accept rules of authority figures and judge actions by their consequences.
- **Conventional level (stages 3 and 4)** Conformity to social rules maintains human relationships and social order.
- **Post-conventional (principled) level (stages 5 and 6)** The individual now defines morality in terms of abstract and universal moral principles.

Research support
The sequence was confirmed by Walker et al. (1987) and Colby et al. (1983) who re-interviewed Kohlberg's original participants at intervals over 20 years.

The link between moral principles and behaviour was supported by ... Kohlberg (1975), who found that only 15% of students at post-conventional level cheated on a test when given the opportunity, compared with 70% at the pre-conventional level.

However, there may be more than one type of morality ... as moral decisions may be based on criteria other than justice. Gilligan (1982) suggested women focus more on 'relationships'.

The theory may be culture-biased because ... although Snarey (1985) confirmed the sequence in 27 countries, other research suggests that post-conventional reasoning is found mainly in industrialised societies.

Limitations
- Kohlberg *underestimated* children's moral understanding (Eisenberg, 1982).
- Kohlberg *overestimated* moral development in adults (Walker et al., 1987).

Theory 2: Eisenberg's (1982) theory

In a nutshell – Young children are able to reason about their own social behaviour and to experience empathy with others' needs.

Distinction between personal distress and empathetic concern depends on the child's ability to adopt another's perspective.

Pro-social dilemmas are those where one's own needs conflict with others' needs; these follow an age-related sequence (Eisenberg et al., 1991).

Levels
1 Self-centred reasoning
2 Needs-oriented reasoning
3 Approval-oriented reasoning
4 Empathetic reasoning
5 Partly internalised principles
6 Strongly internalised principles

Research support for the idea of empathetic concern
Caplan and Hay (1989) found that 3–5-year-olds were often upset by another's distress but rarely offered help. Older children start to take another's perspective (Hughes et al., 1981).

Research support for notion of perspective-taking
Brazilian adolescents with well developed role-taking skills were more compassionate and helpful than poor role-takers (Eisenberg et al., 2001).

Gender and culture differences
- Feshbach (1982) and Eisenberg et al. (1991) found females to be more empathetic than males.
- In *individualist* cultures there are changes from hedonistic to needs-oriented reasoning, but in *collectivist* cultures little needs-orientation is evident.

The relationship between pro-social reasoning and altruism is demonstrated by the fact that ... a child's level of pro-social reasoning predicts altruistic behaviour – Miller et al. (1996) (with pre-school children) and Eisenberg et al. (1991) (with older children).

Probable questions
1. Describe and evaluate **one** theory of moral understanding/pro-social reasoning. *(24 marks)*
2. Outline and evaluate **two** theories of moral understanding/pro-social reasoning. *(24 marks)*

Possible questions
3. (a) Outline **two** theories of moral understanding/pro-social reasoning. *(12 marks)*
   (b) Evaluate **one** of the theories of moral understanding/pro-social reasoning that you outlined in part (a). *(12 marks)*

Chapter 5
Developmental psychology
Cognitive development >

Development of thinking
Development of intelligence
Development of morality >

Theories of moral understanding development
Gender and cultural differences

Gender differences

These reflect different styles of moral understanding rather than a difference in moral competence.

Kohlberg and Kramer (1969) found evidence that women (stage 3) tend to reason at lower levels of moral reasoning than men (stage 4), as they cannot move beyond personal concerns.

Gilligan (1982) found that women use a *morality of care* rather than one based on justice.
There are three stages:
1 Caring for self
2 Caring for others
3 Integration of concern for self and others

Evaluation of Gilligan's studies
- Dilemmas may be more applicable to real-life moral issues than Kohlberg's abstract dilemmas.
- ***But ...*** she used a restricted sample (29 urban, middle-class women) in her original study.
- ***Yet ...*** Gilligan and Attanucci (1988) showed clear gender differences to support this theory.

This research is challenged by ... Walker (1984), who reviewed 79 studies. Only a minority showed significant gender differences in moral reasoning.

Strengths and limitations
- 'Anti-male' agenda may harm males and females (Sommers, 2000).
- Women with a care orientation may also act uncaringly (Durkin, 1995).
- Gilligan showed that moral decisions are based on more than one dimension (i.e. 'different voice' may not necessarily be gender-based).

Explaining gender differences

Interconnectedness
Girls develop a morality of care based on an identification with their mothers whereas boys separate relatively early from this attachment.

Gender differences can be explained by an evolutionary perspective
Taylor *et al.* (2000) argued that differences may be a product of a 'tend and befriend' adaptive response among females.

The notion of interconnectedness is supported by ... Pratt *et al.*'s research (1999). Gilligan claims interconnectedness is greater in girls than boys.

Cultural differences

There is evidence of moral *relativism* rather than moral *universalism*.

Alternative forms of moral reasoning
Miller and Bersoff's study (1992) involved Americans and Asian Indians.

Lying and deception
Triandis (2001) found evidence of a greater tendency towards, and acceptance of, deception in *collectivist* cultures (i.e. it is more acceptable if it helps the ingroup).

Dilemmas used may be culturally biased ... (an imposed etic), which makes comparisons between cultures inappropriate.

Miller and Bersoff also found differences in interpretations of moral issues between the two groups ... **which makes direct comparison of the *level* of moral reasoning difficult.**

Explaining cultural differences

Social complexity There is little evidence of higher-stage moral reasoning in less industrialised societies (Snarey, 1985). It may not be *necessary* in these societies.

Individualist cultures (based on independent self) are more likely to use *justice-based* moral reasoning, whereas *collectivist* cultures (based on interdependent self) are more likely to use *relationship-based* moral reasoning.

An alternative interpretation is that ... differences in social complexity may be related to different *types* rather than *levels* of moral reasoning.

However ... Berry *et al.* (1992) found that moral understanding was more similar across different cultures for *serious* moral issues.

Probable questions
1. Critically consider the influence of gender **and/or** cultural variations on moral understanding/ pro-social reasoning. *(24 marks)*
2. Critically consider the influence of gender **and** cultural variations on moral understanding/ pro-social reasoning. *(24 marks)*

Possible questions
3. Discuss the influence of gender on moral understanding/pro-social reasoning. *(24 marks)*
4. Discuss the influence of cultural variations on moral understanding/pro-social reasoning. *(24 marks)*

Chapter 6 | Personality development | > | Psychodynamic explanations
Developmental psychology | Gender development | | Social learning explanations
Social/personality development > | Adolescence |

In a nutshell – Psychodynamic theories emphasise the constant change and development of the individual. ➤

Limitations of the Freudian view
- It is based on a restricted sample of mainly Viennese women.
- Other equally valid explanations exist for Freud's case studies.
- The theory lacks *falsifiability*.
- The sexual repression of Freud's time may explain the nature of his theory.

Methodological problems include the fact that ... Freud recorded only a few of his case histories. Some (such as the Wolf Man), despite being persuaded at the time, later rejected Freud's interpretations.

Drives

Two basic *drives* motivate all our thoughts and behaviours – *eros* (the life instinct) and *thanatos* (the death instinct).

An alternative view
Neo-Freudians (e.g. Jung and Erikson) adapted Freud's ideas, largely because of his failure to incorporate social and cultural influences.

The structure of personality

In a nutshell – The dynamic interaction between *id*, *ego* and *superego* determines personality.

Tripartite personality
- The *id* aims to get basic needs met, using the pleasure principle to motivate behaviour.
- The *ego's* job is to meet the needs of the id within the constraints of reality (i.e. motivated by the reality principle).
- The *superego* develops as a result of the moral restraints placed on us by our parents.

Ego defence mechanisms
- *Repression* pushes unacceptable id impulses into the unconscious.
- *Projection* involves externalisation of unacceptable wishes onto others.

Levels of consciousness
Everything we are aware of is stored in our conscious mind. Underlying impulses and emotions are stored at an unconscious level.

Supporting evidence
Solms (2000), using evidence from PET scans, has provided some support for a physiological basis for the id and ego.

Supporting evidence
- Evidence of *repression*: Williams' (1994) study of sexually abused women found that one-third had repressed the memory.
- Evidence of *reaction formation*: Adams et al. (1996) found that 80% of homophobics studied were aroused by videos of homosexual sex.

Psychosexual stages

In a nutshell – At any given time the child's libido is focused on the primary erogenous zone for that stage. Frustration and overindulgence may result in *fixation*.

Oral stage (0–18 months) The mouth is the primary focus of libidinal energy. Frustration may result in an 'oral aggressive' character, and overindulgence in an 'oral receptive' character.

Anal stage (18 months–3 years) The focus of pleasure is on eliminating and retaining bodily wastes and represents a conflict between id and ego. Resolution may lead to an 'anal expulsive' or 'anal retentive' character.

Phallic stage (3–6 years) Boys identify with their fathers to escape punishment as a result of their *Oedipus complex*. Girls must resolve their *Electra complex*.

Latency stage (6 years–puberty) Sexual desires and erogenous impulses are repressed and so less dominant.

Genital stage Sexual urges are re-awakened. Interest turns to heterosexual relationships.

Some researchers (Blum and Miller, 1952; Goldberg and Lewis, 1978) have provided **research support** for the link between oral fixation and oral personalities.

But ... others (Fisher and Greenberg, 1996) found no evidence that such a link exists.

Although ... Little Hans provides some confirmation of the existence of a phallic stage, *it does not show us ...* whether the Oedipus complex is universal.

Probable questions
1. Discuss **one or more** psychodynamic explanation(s) of personality development. *(24 marks)*
2. Discuss **two** explanations of personality development. *(24 marks)*

Possible questions
3. Outline and evaluate **two** psychodynamic explanations of personality development. *(24 marks)*

Chapter 6	Personality development	>	Psychodynamic explanations
Developmental psychology	Gender development		Social learning explanations
Social/personality development >	Adolescence		

Explanation 1: Bandura's (1991) social–cognitive theory

In a nutshell – The acquisition of everything that makes up our personality can be explained using social learning principles.

Reciprocal determinism
The environment and a person's behaviour influence each other.

Stages in the modelling process
- **Attention** To learn anything, a child must pay attention.
- **Retention** The model's actions are stored as mental images.
- **Reproduction** Images are translated into behaviour.
- **Motivation** Child must be motivated to reproduce behaviour.

Self-regulation
We constantly monitor and evaluate our behaviour to see how well it fits internal and external standards, using 3 steps:
- Self-observation
- Judgement
- Self-response

Self-efficacy
The more confident an individual is in their own abilities, the more likely he or she is to engage in that behaviour. We are influenced by the successful performance of a behaviour and by vicarious experiences.

Strengths and limitations
- Bandura's theory has generated applications such as using self-efficacy in health and sporting behaviour.
- However, it focuses too much on the situation, underestimating importance of inner personality traits.

Research support
Bandura *et al.* (1961) found that children imitated both specific and general acts of aggression, and that modelling may result in direct or vicarious learning.

Applications of this theory include ... self-control therapy. Self-regulation is an important part of this therapy, which involves the use of *behavioural charts, environmental planning* and *self-contracts*.

Research support
- **Direct reinforcement** Feltz (1982) found that self-efficacy was raised in athletes by showing them edited videotapes of their performance.
- **Indirect reinforcement** Schunk (1983) found that American school pupils who were told that their peers had done well on a test also did well.
- **Verbal instruction** Blittner *et al.* (1978) found that participants were more likely to give up smoking when told they had scored highly on personal control and willpower.

Explanation 2: Mischel's person–situation theory (1968)

In a nutshell – Although there is some consistency in behaviour across situations, this can not be explained by broad personality traits.

Behaviour specificity
Our behaviour is determined by the specific situation in which we find ourselves.

Person variables
These are based on past experience, and determine which stimuli are perceived and acted upon:
- Competencies
- Encoding strategies and personal constructs
- Expectations
- Subjective values
- Self-regulatory systems and plans

Evidence for specificity
Hartshorne and May (1928–30) found that willingness to cheat varied across situations, but people do appear to behave consistently on some forms of moral behaviour (Burton, 1976).

Evidence for behaviour consistency
Claims about lack of consistency across situations have been supported (e.g. Mischel and Peake, 1982), **but ...** other researchers have found that personality traits are consistent *on average* (Epstein, 1979).

Evidence for individual/situation interaction
Shoda *et al.* (1994) showed that individuals may have the same personality as each other but behave quite differently in specific situations.

Probable questions
1. Discuss **one or more** social learning explanations of personality development. *(24 marks)*
2. Outline and evaluate the social learning **and** psychodynamic approaches to personality development. *(24 marks)*

Possible questions
3. Compare and contrast the social learning and psychodynamic explanations of personality development. *(24 marks)*

Chapter 6
Developmental psychology
Social/personality development
>

Personality development
Gender development   >
Adolescence

Explanations of gender identity/gender roles

Explanation 1: Social cognitive theory (Bandura, 1991)

In a nutshell – Gender-role behaviours are acquired through differential reinforcement and observational learning.

Modelling
Children must have the ability to:
- class males and females into distinct groups
- recognise similarities in their behaviour
- store these behaviours as abstractions in memory
- use these to guide their own behaviour.

Enactive experience and differential reinforcement
- Children begin producing behaviour that is socially linked to gender and as a result experience social reactions from those around them.
- They extract and weigh up the diverse outcome information to construct their conception of gender-appropriate conduct.

Direct tuition
As children acquire linguistic skills, direct tuition serves to inform children about different styles of conduct and how they are linked to gender.

Supported by ... Perry and Bussey (1979), who found that children imitated behaviour of a same-sex model if the behaviour didn't contradict existing gender stereotypes.

Research support
- Smith and Lloyd (1978) studied mothers playing with an infant. They found evidence of differential reinforcement of gender-role behaviour.
- Fagot *et al.* (1992) showed that parents with the clearest patterns of differential reinforcement had children with the strongest gender preferences.

Direct instruction versus modelling influences
Research (e.g. Barkley *et al.*, 1977) has shown that labelling (direct instruction) was *more influential* than same-sex behaviour (modelling) among pre-school children.

Evaluation of Bandura's theory
- It is a 'developmental' theory – i.e. the processes of learning are the same at any age.
- The theory portrays the child as passive in development, **but this overlooks** the importance of self-evaluation and self-regulation in development.

Explanation 2: Gender schema theory (Martin and Halverson, 1981)

In a nutshell – As soon as children have a basic gender identity, they look increasingly to the environment for information to enrich their gender schema.

Ingroup and outgroup schema
As soon as children acquire a basic gender identity, they think of their own sex as the 'ingroup' and the other sex as the 'outgroup', concentrating on learning activities in the ingroup.

Peer relationships
Children are more positive towards and seek out others of the same sex as they are 'like me' and avoid members of the opposite sex as they are 'not like me'.

Bem (1981)
Children who are 'gender schematic' encode information in ways that reflect current gender stereotypes. Non-schematic children develop a more androgynous gender schema.

Research support
- Martin and Halverson (1983) found that children under 6 paid more attention to and recalled more gender-consistent than gender-inconsistent information.
- Bradbard *et al.* (1986) found that young children paid greater attention to ingroup than outgroup schemas.

This theory explains why ... gender stereotypes are resistant to change and why many children are highly sexist, because they actively seek to acquire gender-appropriate schema.

Biology offers an alternative explanation
Money and Ehrhardt (1972) claimed gender identity was entirely *social*, **but** eventually their twin study demonstrated that *biological* sex may be fundamental to gender identity.

Probable questions
1. Describe and evaluate **one** explanation of the development of gender identity/gender roles. *(24 marks)*
2. Outline and evaluate **two** explanations of the development of gender identity/gender roles. *(24 marks)*

Possible questions
3. (a) Describe **one** explanation of the development of gender identity/gender roles. *(12 marks)*

   (b) To what extent is the explanation of the development of gender identity/gender roles you described in (a) supported by research studies? *(12 marks)*

47

Chapter 6	Personality development	Social development in adolescence
Developmental psychology	Gender development	Relationships with parents and peers
Social/personality development >	Adolescence >	Cultural differences in adolescent behaviour

Theory 1: Erikson's psychosocial theory

In a nutshell – The central task of adolescence is the achievement of a mature adult identity.

The eight stages of life
Each stage has its own task or 'crisis'. During adolescence, children face an identity crisis as they struggle to establish who they are and where they are going.

Identity formation
To achieve an identity, adolescents must:
- establish trust
- establish autonomy
- take the initiative
- be industrious.

Identity confusion
This arises from failure to commit to definite life choices, leading to a period of indecision and identity *diffusion*.
- Problems with intimacy
- Negative identity
- Diffusion of time perspective
- Diffusion of industry

Research support ... for these eight stages came from Erikson's work as a psychoanalyst, and through his interviews with Dakota Indians.

A consequence of identity formation is ... the ability to form intimate relationships (supported by Kahn *et al.*, 1985).

However ... there may be evidence of *gender bias* in this theory (female identity requires the development of an intimate relationship) and *cultural bias* (identity formation may be relevant only to industrialised societies).

Challenges to 'adolescence as crisis'
Some research suggests adolescence is no more stressful than other times of life (Siddique and D'Arcy, 1984) and the 'turmoil' view of adolescence was a product of early research with mainly abnormal populations.

The theory was influential because ... it introduced the idea of lifespan development.

But it is difficult to test ... as some concepts are vague.

Research evidence: Marcia (1966)

Marcia operationalised Erikson's theory by interviewing adolescents experiencing an identity crisis. Marcia's research showed that the attainment of a mature identity depended on *crisis/exploration* and *commitment*.

Four identity statuses
Marcia found evidence of four identity 'statuses' that adolescents go through (only moratorium is essential for identity achievement):
- Identity diffusion
- Identity foreclosure
- Moratorium
- Identity achievement

However ... research (e.g. Meilman, 1979) suggests that identity achievement comes later than predicted and may not be permanent.

Research support ... exists for the *description* of developmental statuses (Kroger, 1996) and their *sequence* (Waterman, 1985).

Strengths and limitations of the research
Marcia's research provides a useful categorisation of adolescents.
But ... the sample may not have been representative and subjects may have provided socially desirable answers.

Theory 2: Coleman's focal theory

In a nutshell – Many adolescents experience no significant turmoil because they have to focus on only one significant issue at a time.

Focal issues and development
Coleman (1990) argued that concerns about different issues peaked at different points during adolescence rather than being concentrated at one time.

Stress and adaptation
Adolescents who must deal with more than one issue at a time experience an increase in stress, which may lead to psychological problems.

Research support for this theory ... comes from Coleman and Hendry (1990) and Simmons and Blyth (1987).

This theory explains ... why some adolescents cope and others fail to adapt, despite having a similar number of crises – because they have an *active* role in their development.

Probable questions
1. Discuss research (theories **and/or** studies) into social development in adolescence. *(24 marks)*
2. Discuss research (theories **and/or** studies) into the formation of identity in adolescence. *(24 marks)*

Possible questions
3. (a) Outline research into social development in adolescence. *(12 marks)*
   (b) To what extent do relationships with parents **and/or** peers influence this process? *(12 marks)*

Chapter 6 | | Personality development | Social development in adolescence
Developmental psychology | | Gender development | **Relationships with parents and peers**
Social/personality development | Adolescence | > | Cultural differences in adolescent behaviour

Relationships with parents

Adolescence is characterised by a movement away from parents towards autonomy and independence.

Changes in parent relationships
With the advent of formal operational thinking, adolescents begin to view their attachment relationships more objectively.

Developing autonomy
Adolescents still turn to parents in times of stress, but the exploratory urge takes on much greater importance.

Formal operational thinking
This assumes all adolescents reach this stage, but Dasen (1994) claims that only a third of adults ever reach this stage, and even then not during adolescence.

Although autonomy is important ... warm and close parental relationships are important too.

Supported by ... research by Larson et al. (1996), who found that time spent with each parent individually remained consistent in early adolescence.

Studies of parent relationships

Frey and Rothlisberger (1996) found that adolescents had twice as many relationships with peers as family. Parental relationships were more important for boys than girls.

Parent–adolescent relationship
Allen and Land (1999) found that adolescents who lacked secure feelings towards parents were 'handicapped' (expected relationships not to work).

However ... the reverse relationship is also valuable, as fathers' relationships with their children can have a positive effect on their psychological health (Montemayor et al., 1993).

The claim that warm, supportive parenting is best is *backed up by research* on parenting styles (e.g. Steinberg et al., 1991).

However ... most research is conducted on US and European adolescents, which may not tell us what adolescence is like in all cultures.

Relationships with peers

Peers take on many of the functions that they will serve for the rest of an individual's life.

Importance of peers (Ainsworth, 1989)
• Important sources of intimacy
• Feedback on social behaviour
• Source of social influence

Peer conformity
This is strong in mid-adolescence, and then declines. It reflects adolescents' attempts to orient themselves toward adulthood.

Peer attachments are different *from parental attachments ...* i.e. more symmetrical and less critical. Parental attachments change to become more like peer relationships.

This can be explained by ... the decline in peer conformity because there is more interest in romantic relationships after mid-adolescence.

Studies of peer relationships

Self-esteem
Bishop and Inderbitzen (1995) found that students with at least one reciprocal friend had significantly higher self-esteem scores than those without.

Differences
Frey and Rothlisberger (1996) found that girls had a larger number of confidential and more intense relationships than did boys.

Supported by ... Bagwell et al. (1998), who found that adults who had a close friend at school experienced better overall adjustment later on.

It is possible that ... girls have more intimate relationships because they rely more on social support than boys.

Probable questions

1. Critically consider research (theories **and/or** studies) into relationships with parents and/or peers during adolescence. *(24 marks)*

2. (a) Describe research (theories **and/or** studies) into social development in adolescence. *(12 marks)*

   (b) To what extent do relationships with parents **and/or** peers influence this development? *(12 marks)*

Possible questions

3. Discuss research (theories **and/or** studies) into relationships with parents during adolescence. *(24 marks)*

4. Discuss research (theories **and/or** studies) into relationships with peers during adolescence. *(24 marks)*

Chapter 6
Developmental psychology
Social/personality development >

Personality development
Gender development
Adolescence   >

Social development in adolescence
Relationships with parents and peers
Cultural differences in adolescent behaviour

Culture and adolescence

Not all cultures are the same; therefore we might expect many differences in how adolescence is viewed in Western and non-Western cultures.

Achievement
Individuals from individualist cultures are more achievement-oriented than those from collectivist cultures. Kagen and Madsen (1972) found Anglo-American adolescents more competitive than Mexican counterparts.

Sexuality
Adolescents in the remote Irish community of Ines Baeg were found to be sexually naïve, whereas the Mangaia of Polynesia are encouraged to explore their sexuality during adolescence.

Rites of passage
Some societies have elaborate rituals that mark a child's passage into adulthood. In the West, there are no dramatic rituals, which makes the attainment of adult status ambiguous.

Criticism of individualism/collectivism distinction
Stevenson (1995) found that Japan and China (both collectivist cultures) are both very much achievement-oriented.

There are also historical differences
Within our own society, there have been changes over time in the degree to which adolescent sexuality has been considered 'normal'.

However ... children attain different forms of 'adult' status at different ages, meaning there is no one culturally defined point at which they reach 'adulthood'.

Supported by ... Mead (1928), who found the passage from childhood to adulthood to be relatively easy in Samoa, compared with Western cultures.

However ... other anthropologists are divided over whether Mead's conclusions were a valid reflection of growing up in Samoa.

Subculture and adolescence

A 'subculture' shares many of the characteristics of the dominant culture but may also have characteristics that are peculiar to it.

Ethnicity and achievement
Education and achievement are more highly valued among some ethnic groups than others (DES, 2003).

Identity formation
It is difficult for members of ethnic minority groups as the values and conventions of the wider society may clash with those of the home background. Phinney (1993) suggested there are three stages in the development of ethnic identity ('unexamined', 'searchers' and 'resolution').

Family background
Low SES adolescents have parents who place greater value on external (e.g. obedience) rather than internal (e.g. self-reliance) characteristics.

Poverty and adolescence
Duncan et al. (1994) found that adolescents who experienced persistent poverty had lower IQs and a higher likelihood of behavioural problems.

Phinney's model is criticised by ... Berry (1997), who claimed that successful identity formation requires both retention of cultural traditions and the formation of relationships within the larger society.

Supported by ... a study which found that immigrant students in Canada frequently did better at school and showed less anti-social behaviour (Berry, 1997).

Although ... internal control (high SES (socioeconomic status) adolescents) is associated with higher IQ.
It is also associated with ... a higher incidence of drug use (Hendry et al., 1993).

However ... research on this relationship is inevitably correlational, yet causal conclusions are often suggested.

Probable questions

1. Discuss research (theories **and/or** studies) into cultural differences in adolescent behaviour. *(24 marks)*

2. (a) Describe research (theories **and/or** studies) into social development in adolescence. *(12 marks)*

   (b) To what extent are there cultural differences in adolescent behaviour? *(12 marks)*

Possible questions

3. Describe and evaluate research (theories **and/or** studies) into cultural differences in adolescent behaviour. *(24 marks)*

chapter 7
omparative psychology
Evolutionary explanations >

Human reproductive behaviour >
Evolution of mental disorders
Evolution of intelligence

Sexual selection and human reproduction
Evolutionary explanations of parental investment

Nature of sexual selection

Any trait that increases the reproductive success of an individual will become more and more exaggerated over evolutionary time.

Gender-specific criteria
Human females make a greater investment in their offspring (gestation and infant care) so are choosey when selecting a partner. Males must therefore compete with each other to be chosen.

Origins of mate preferences
Current mate preferences exist as evolved psychological mechanisms that originally solved the problem of mate choice in the EEA. These preferences bias mating in favour of individuals with those characteristics.

Supporting evidence
- A study of 37 cultures (Buss, 1989) showed universal mate preferences for males and females.
- A study of women seeking sperm donors showed that they made their choices according to evolutionary predictions (Scheib, 1994).

However ... although males value attractiveness in potential mates, the specific details are also predictable from cultural norms and change across time.

This view of sexual attraction cannot explain ... attraction in partners who have *no interest in reproductive potential* (e.g. homosexual relationships).

The idea that human behaviour can be explained in terms of the selective pressures operating in the EEA is **not universally accepted**, as it ignores the importance of *cultural* evolution since that time.

Forms of sexual selection

Sexual selection may influence the development of physical and behavioural *indicators* of desirable traits, and characteristics that are a response to sperm *competition*.

Physical and behavioural indicators
Human beings are pre-programmed to attend to displays of important physical and behavioural indicators (relevant to 'good genes' and 'good parenting') and are more willing to mate with those who possess them.

Sperm competition
Research on comparative testicle size in primate species (Baker and Bellis, 1995) suggests ancestral human females in the EEA must have had multiple partners.

However, although ... indicators represent good genetic quality they can be faked.

On the other hand ... facial symmetry is an honest signal because it is physiologically difficult to achieve and (virtually) impossible to fake.

The idea that humans are by nature promiscuous is **supported by research** (e.g. Betzig, 1993; Baker and Bellis, 1995).

Consequences of sexual selection

The selective pressures on males and females have led to different physical and behavioural consequences for each sex.

Physical characteristics
- In species where females must choose males, this leads to *sexual dimorphism*, as males compete to be selected.
- Facial characteristics such as *neotony* (in females) and *facial symmetry* are important indicators of reproductive capacity and/or quality.

Human mental evolution
Mate choices in the EEA may have led to the evolution of *neophilia* (love of novelty and creativity), *intelligence* and *language*, which would help in the selection of a suitable mate.

Commentary on the evolutionary approach
Dawkins (1976) believes that humans, with their large brains and intelligence, are in a position to depart from the dictates of their evolutionary past, rather than having their behaviour *determined* by pressures that are no longer relevant.

Probable questions
1. Discuss the relationship between sexual selection and human reproductive behaviour. *(24 marks)*
2. Discuss evolutionary explanations of human reproductive behaviour. *(24 marks)*

Possible questions
3. Discuss the relationship between sexual selection and **two** areas of human reproductive behaviour. *(24 marks)*

Chapter 7	Human reproductive behaviour >	Sexual selection and human reproduction
Comparative psychology	Evolution of mental disorders	Evolutionary explanations of parental investment
Evolutionary explanations >	Evolution of intelligence	

Parental investment theory (Trivers, 1972)

Female investment is greater because eggs are more costly than sperm. Males compete for *quantity* of females, and females select for *quality* of males and their resources.

Supported by ... Smith (1984) who found that 80% of cultures are polygynous, consistent with the claim that men have more to gain from this mating arrangement.

However ... reproduction rate in Western cultures is *lowest* among the wealthiest people, which challenges the view that resources and reproductive success are linked.

Sex differences

Maternal investment
Human mothers make a greater *prenatal* contribution of resources (through pregnancy) and a greater *postnatal* contribution (through breastfeeding). As a result, the costs of random mating would be high for human females.

Paternal investment
Males expend a large part of their reproductive effort on courtship and mating, and relatively little on parental care.

Sexual jealousy
This may have evolved as a solution to the problems of *cuckoldry* (for males) and *loss of resources* (for females).

Consequences of the high cost of maternal investment
- Infant dependency means that females want male providers.
- The expense of childrearing means that females want to ensure good quality offspring and thus a good quality mate.

Research support
- Buss et al. (1992) found that male students indicated more concern about sexual infidelity (possibility of cuckoldry) and females about emotional infidelity (possible loss of resources).
- Many cultures have social practices that are aimed at reducing the chance of female infidelity.

However, women do not always select and men compete
In some cases (e.g. among the Ache Indians), a surplus of women has led to greater competition among women and increased extramarital affairs.

In humans, shared care is important ... because of the high cost of childrearing human males tend to restrict their reproductive opportunities and invest more in each individual offspring. This results in greater selectivity in males (e.g. for attractive females).

Parent–offspring conflict

In a nutshell – Resource allocations that maximise parental fitness are not identical to those which maximise *offspring* fitness – resulting in conflict.

Trivers (1974)
- Parents and offspring will be in conflict over *when* weaning should finish.
- Parents should encourage children to value siblings.
- Parents will punish conflict and reward co-operation between siblings.

Sibling rivalry
This may develop as individual offspring try to maximise their own fitness by taking more than their 'fair share' of parental resources.

Conflict before birth
High blood pressure during pregnancy is caused by the foetus secreting hormones when it perceives the need for more nutrition.

Conflict after birth
Conflict with a current child is most intense when parents attempt to maximise their own fitness by transferring resources to a younger offspring.

An alternative strategy
Lalumière et al. (1996) suggest that parents tend to steer siblings along *different* developmental paths, thus reducing competition for the same resources.

Mothers with higher blood pressure have larger babies and fewer spontaneous abortions (Haig, 1993) ... *therefore this is an adaptive strategy.*

However ... Salmon and Daly (1998) suggest that younger children do not compete, but instead form alliances to gain access to resources.

Probable questions
1. Critically consider evolutionary explanations of parental investment. (24 marks)
2. Discuss the relationship between sexual selection and parental investment. (24 marks)

Possible questions
3. (a) Outline and evaluate the relationship between sexual selection and human reproductive behaviour. (12 marks)
   (b) Outline and evaluate evolutionary explanations of parental investment. (12 marks)

hapter 7
omparative psychology
Evolutionary explanations >

Human reproductive behaviour
Evolution of mental disorders
Evolution of intelligence

Evolutionary explanations of depression
Evolutionary explanations of anxiety disorders

Bipolar disorder (BD)

Bipolar disorder is a disorder marked by alternating periods of mania and depression.

Reproductive fitness
If possession of bipolar genes were advantageous to our ancestors, this would cause individuals with those genes to be favoured in subsequent generations.

EOBD hypothesis (Sherman, 2001)
Bipolar behaviours are viewed as adaptations to the selective pressures of long, severe winters and short summers.

- **Cold-adapted physique** BD is associated with a *pyknic* physique, which would have helped conserve heat in conditions of extreme cold.

- **Hibernation** Similarities between BD and the cycle of hibernation suggest that both evolved in response to environmental adversity.

- **Adaptive significance** The depression phase of BD would preserve group harmony and conserve energy in the long winter months, and the mania phase would be adaptive for emergencies.

Genetic evidence
Evidence exists for an inherited basis for BD (Nesse, 1999) although BD is not entirely due to genetic factors. Research suggests there is most likely to be a number of genes contributing to BD, supporting the reproductive fitness argument.

Neurophysiological evidence
Previc (2002) queries the lack of a neurophysiological basis for this model.
But ... research evidence (Arbisi et al., 1994) shows that dopamine levels fluctuate seasonally.

The EOBD hypothesis makes sense because ... of the need to balance energy expenditure with seasonal fluctuations in food availability which would have been essential for survival in the EEA.

This explanation can be applied to ... evolutionary psychiatry, suggesting that we can make sense of disorders by considering the meaning of behaviours in both their current and adaptive origins.

Unipolar disorder

Unipolar disorder is a disorder marked by lowering of mood and disturbances of sleep, concentration and appetite.

Social competition hypothesis
- Depression is an adaptive response to losing rank in a status conflict and seeing oneself as a loser. This prevents further injury and preserves the stability of the social group.

- In the modern world the depressive response may be triggered by other loss situations but this response is *maladaptive*. This can be explained by the concept of *genome lag*.

Defection hypothesis
Post-partum depression (PPD) was an adaptive response because it led women to limit their investment in a child in unfavourable conditions that might reduce their overall reproductive success.

Supported by ... Gilbert and Allan (1998) who found a significant correlation between depression and measures of entrapment and defeat.

A variation to this hypothesis
Rank theory suggests that conflict results in either the *yielding* (akin to depression) or winning (akin to mania) subroutines.

Predictions supported by research
- Lack of social support predicts onset of PPD (Gotlib et al., 1991).

- Impoverished environment is a significant risk factor (Warner et al., 1996).

- PPD results in loss of interest in the child (Beck, 1992).

- PPD leads to increased investment by fathers (Hagen, 2002).

Probable questions

1. Critically consider **one or more** explanations of depression from an evolutionary perspective. *(24 marks)*

2. Critically consider explanations of **two** types of mental disorder from an evolutionary perspective. *(24 marks)*

Possible questions

3. Describe and evaluate **one** explanation of depression from an evolutionary perspective. *(24 marks)*

53

Chapter 7	Human reproductive behaviour	Evolutionary explanations of depression
Comparative psychology	Evolution of mental disorders >	Evolutionary explanations of anxiety disorders
Evolutionary explanations >	Evolution of intelligence	

Nature of anxiety

Anxiety may have been useful to our ancestors, but excessive anxiety is clearly disabling.

Types
General anxiety evolved as an emotional response to situations where the specific threat cannot be identified. *Specific* anxiety evolved to protect individuals against a particular type of danger.

A protective response
Anxiety can give rise to a specialised response to specific dangers:
• Escape or avoidance
• Aggressive defence
• Freezing/immobility
• Submission/appeasement

Subtypes
Subtypes of anxiety have evolved to defend the individual against particular types of threat.
• **Fear** Responding to threats with fear is clearly linked to survival (e.g. heights induce freezing).
• **Obsessive–compulsive behaviours** Ritual behaviours (e.g. grooming behaviour) associated with this type of anxiety disorder can be considered an exaggeration of mechanisms that drive more adaptive behaviour.

However ... Nesse (2005) suggests that anxiety is a *useful* state shaped by natural selection which increases our ability to cope with the adaptive challenges that arise in specific situations.

Adaptiveness of anxiety is illustrated by ... the fact that people who have their adrenal glands removed would die without supplements of adrenaline (produced as a response to stress).

Supported by ... research from Kendler *et al.* (1992) and Nestadt *et al.* (2000) showing that anxiety disorders are largely a product of genetic factors.

Evolution of anxiety disorders

Anxiety is thought to have evolved as an emotional response increasing our ability to cope with threats in our environment.

Ancient fears
Some stimuli (e.g. snakes, heights) reflected very real fears to our ancestors. Most modern-day phobias are exaggerations of these ancient fears.

Preparedness
Seligman (1970) proposed that animals are biologically prepared to rapidly learn an association between particular stimuli and fear, one which it is difficult to extinguish.

Prepotency
Natural selection has shaped our nervous systems so that we attend more to certain cues (e.g. sudden noises) than others.

Supported by ... Öhman and Soares (1994), who provided evidence that important components of phobic responses are set in motion before the phobic stimulus is represented in awareness.

Evidence for preparedness
McNally (1987) found firm evidence for the prediction that some fears are harder to unlearn but *not* that they are easier to learn in the first place.

An alternative explanation ... is the notion of 'expectancy bias' (Davey, 1995), which means that there is no need to consider evolutionary history in the development of phobias.

This may not be relevant to an understanding of clinical phobias because ... research has tended to focus on avoidance responses rather than clinical disorders. Merckelbach *et al.* (1988) suggested that clinical disorders tend to be 'non-prepared' and do not show characteristics of prepared behaviours.

Probable questions
1. Critically consider **one or more** explanations of anxiety disorders from an evolutionary perspective. *(24 marks)*
2. (a) Outline and evaluate **one or more** explanations of anxiety disorders from an evolutionary perspective. *(12 marks)*
   (b) Outline and evaluate **one or more** explanations of depression from an evolutionary perspective. *(12 marks)*

Possible questions
3. Discuss the explanation of **two** types of anxiety disorder from an evolutionary perspective. *(24 marks)*

Chapter 7
Comparative psychology
Evolutionary explanations >

Human reproductive behaviour
Evolution of mental disorders
Evolution of intelligence >

Evolutionary factors in human intelligence
Relationship between brain size and intelligence

Factor 1: Foraging demands

Most explanations of the evolution of intelligence have focused on the demand of the physical environment, particularly problems with finding food.

Finding food
Dunbar (1992) suggests that intelligence evolved because of an increased cognitive demand on *frugivores* (including hominids) to monitor a widely dispersed food supply.

Extracting food: tool use
Mercader *et al.* (2002) believe that comparative evidence from studies of chimpanzees and archaeological studies of early humans suggest that tool use is an indication of intelligence in both species.

Research support
Only the great apes appear to have the sophistication of understanding necessary for tool use, which supports a link between tool use and intelligence.

Cause or effect?
The fact that an animal uses tools does not tell us whether this is a *cause* or an *effect* of intelligence. Byrne (1995) suggests that tool use is simply a byproduct of other abilities, i.e. it is an *effect* rather than a *cause*.

Factor 2: Social theories

Individuals who can best deal with the demands of living in large and complex social groups and can use this to their advantage would be more successful.

Machiavellian intelligence (Whiten and Byrne, 1988)
Those individuals able to use and exploit others in their social group without causing aggression would be favoured.

Meat-sharing hypothesis (Stanford, 1999)
The strategic sharing of meat (to forge alliances and persuade females to mate) may have paved the way for human intelligence. It requires considerable cognitive abilities to recognise individuals with whom meat has been shared.

Supported by ... Byrne and Whiten (1992), who found a strong positive correlation between a species' amount of tactical deception and neocortical size.

However ... Cosmides (1989) provides an alternative explanation, arguing that human intelligence is specially adapted to deal with social problem-solving because people solve such problems more easily than abstract ones.

Studies of human societies confirm the 'meat for sex' hypothesis (e.g. study of the Ache of Paraguay – Hill and Kaplan, 1988), as do studies of chimpanzees (Gilby, 2001).

However ... Mitani and Watts (2001) disagree with this hypothesis, arguing that male chimps are more likely to share meat with other males (for alliances) than with females (for sex).

Foraging versus social theories
- Dunbar (1992) found a positive relationship between *group* size and *neocortex ratio* but no relationship between *environmental* complexity and *neocortex ratio*, thus upholding a *social* origin of primate intelligence.
- Byrne (1995) suggests that differences between apes (and therefore humans) and monkeys may reflect differences in the environmental challenges faced by these species.

Factor 3: Language

Only humans have developed the capacity for language, which may be the impetus for the evolution of intelligence.
Other species show the *precursors* of language or can be taught elements of human language, suggesting similarity between closely related species.

Human language is probably the *outcome* rather than the *cause* of intelligence, but once evolved would have a significant effect on further development of intelligence.

Probable questions

1. Critically consider evolutionary factors in the development of human intelligence. *(24 marks)*
2. Discuss **two** evolutionary factors in the development of human intelligence. *(24 marks)*

Possible questions

3. Discuss the evolution of human intelligence. *(24 marks)*

Chapter 7
Comparative psychology
Evolutionary explanations   >

Human reproductive behaviour
Evolution of mental disorders
Evolution of intelligence   >

Evolutionary factors in human intelligence
Relationship between brain size and intelligence

Comparative studies of brain size and intelligence

Comparative studies of other animals enable us to examine species with a wide variety of brain sizes and widely differing levels of intelligence.

Brain quantity
- **Absolute brain size** Species with the biggest bodies tend to have the biggest brains, which are needed to control and maintain a larger body.
- **Brain–body ratio** Higher EQ quotients indicate species (e.g. humans) with larger than expected brain size related to body size.

Brain quality
Some researchers (e.g. Holloway, 1979) believe that brain *quality* (particularly the growth of the neocortex in mammals) is the most important factor in the growth of intelligence.

However ... the relationship between EQ and intelligence has not been supported by research (e.g. Macphail, 1982), although there are difficulties in making comparative estimates of intelligence.

Also ... it is difficult to establish a reliable correlation between EQ and intelligence because animals vary extensively in body and brain weight at different times of the year and at different periods of life and between sexes.

Herman (1986) disagrees with the idea that ... cetaceans have lower intelligence – their brains may have fewer neocortical levels but neural density and size of frontal lobes are similar to those of humans.

Human studies

Large brains are thought to give humans a significant advantage in terms of evolutionary fitness.

Brain size
- **Head size and IQ** Wickett et al. (1994) found that in 25 studies, the majority obtained correlations between 0.1 and 0.3 for head size and IQ.
- **Studies using MRI scans** (e.g. Andreasen et al., 1993) have found significant correlations between brain size and intelligence.

Brain structure
- **Cortical neurons** Haig (1987) estimated a correlation of 0.48 between brain size and cortical neurons (indicates cognitive ability).
- **Grey matter and IQ** Thompson et al. (2001) claimed that grey matter is highly heritable and is an important determinant of IQ.

Sex differences
Several studies (e.g. Ankey, 1992; Rushton, 1992) have found that male brains are heavier than female brains or that the cranial capacity of males is greater.

Problems with the brain size/intelligence relationship
- Correlations may be significant, but not highly, so may be essentially meaningless.
- Correlations do not imply causality, so a third variable (such as good diet) might be involved.
- Studies of microcephalics (e.g. Sassman and Zartler, 1982) have found many to have a relatively normal IQ.
- Brain size may instead be related to *expertise* (more significant to survival) rather than IQ.
- Giedd et al. (1996) found wide variations of brain size in people with *normal* IQ.

Supported by ... Diamond (1991), who found that animals reared in enriched environments have more cortical neurons.

However ... the development of grey matter has been shown to be affected by both genetic *and* environmental factors (Storfer, 2001).

This cannot explain ... the paradox that despite differences in brain size, male and female IQ levels are the same.

Probable questions
1. Discuss the relationship between brain size and intelligence. *(24 marks)*
2. Describe and evaluate research (theories **and/or** studies) of the relationship between brain size and intelligence. *(24 marks)*

Possible questions
3. (a) Outline evolutionary factors in the development of human intelligence. *(12 marks)*
   (b) To what extent has research supported the claim that there is a relationship between brain size and intelligence? *(12 marks)*

Chapter 8 | Schizophrenia, depression, anxiety > | **Clinical characteristics**

Individual differences

Psychopathology >

Schizophrenia

Depression

Anxiety disorders

Schizophrenia

In a nutshell – Schizophrenia is a serious mental disorder characterised by a profound disruption in cognition and emotion.

The nature of schizophrenia

Note that schizophrenia is *not* a 'split' or 'multiple' personality, nor are schizophrenics perpetually incoherent nor do they constantly display psychotic behaviour.

- **Positive symptoms** reflect a distortion of normal functioning.
- **Negative symptoms** reflect a loss of normal functioning.

Diagnostic criteria

Under DSM-IVR, a diagnosis of schizophrenia requires 2 or more positive symptoms for a period of at least 1 month.

Positive symptoms

Positive symptoms of schizophrenia include the following:

- Delusions
- Experiences of being controlled
- Auditory hallucinations
- Disordered thinking

Negative symptoms

Negative symptoms of schizophrenia include the following:

- Affective flattening
- Alogia
- Avolition

Depression

In a nutshell – Depression is a low emotional state characterised by significant levels of sadness, lack of energy and poor self-worth, and feelings of guilt.

The nature of depression

Depression is classified as a *mood disorder* on DSM-IVR. Mood disorders such as depression affect a person's emotional state.

- In *unipolar disorder* people suffer from a prolonged low emotional state without an alternating state of mania. As with bipolar disorder, there may be periods of normality in between episodes.
- In *bipolar disorder* there are alternating states of mania and depression.

Diagnostic criteria

Under DSM-IVR, a diagnosis of depression requires the presence of a sad, *depressed mood*, plus 4 (from 8) other criteria including the following:

- Difficulty in sleeping
- Loss of energy
- Recurrent thoughts of death or suicide

Anxiety disorder: Obsessive–compulsive behaviour (OCD)

In a nutshell – OCD is characterised by excessive, intrusive and inappropriate obsessions or compulsions.

The nature of OCD

OCD is an anxiety disorder, and so is characterised by extreme or pathological anxiety as its principal mood disturbance.

- **Obsessions** These are recurrent, intrusive thoughts or impulses that produce anxiety because they are unlike a person's usual thoughts.
- **Compulsions** These are repetitive behaviours or mental acts that reduce the anxiety accompanying an obsession. As an individual recognises that these are unreasonable, obsessions also *create* anxiety.

Diagnostic criteria

Under DSM-IVR, a diagnosis of OCD is given if an individual:

- Experiences recurrent and persistent thoughts or impulses that cause anxiety.
- Displays repetitive behaviours that they feel driven to perform in response.
- Recognises that these are excessive or unreasonable.

Probable questions

1. (a) Outline **two or more** clinical characteristics of schizophrenia. (5 marks)

   (b) Discuss **two or more** biological explanations of schizophrenia. (25 marks)

2. (a) Outline **two or more** clinical characteristics of depression. (5 marks)

   (b) Discuss **two or more** explanations of depression. (25 marks)

3. (a) Outline **two or more** clinical characteristics of any **one** anxiety disorder. (5 marks)

   (b) Discuss **two or more** psychological explanations of any **one** anxiety disorder. (25 marks)

Chapter 8
Individual differences
Psychopathology >

Schizophrenia, depression, anxiety
Schizophrenia >
Depression
Anxiety disorders

Biological explanations of schizophrenia
Psychological explanations of schizophrenia

Genetic factors

The finding that schizophrenia runs in families suggests that gene(s) are responsible for the disorder.

Biological relatives Schizophrenia is more common in close biological relatives of a schizophrenic (Gottesman, 1991).

Twin studies Identical twins have 48% risk of developing schizophrenia compared to 17% for non-identical twins (Janicak *et al.*, 2001).

Adoption studies 14% of biological relatives of schizophrenic adoptees were schizophrenic, and only 2.7% of adoptive relatives (Kety *et al.*, 1988).

Molecular biology Miyakawa *et al.* (2003) found schizophrenics more likely to have a defective version of the gene PPP3CC, associated with *calcineurin*.

Limitations of genetic explanation
- There is a lower than 50% risk of an identical twin developing the disorder if the co-twin (who shares the same genes) is already schizophrenic. **This suggests that** ... genetics is not the only contributing factor.
- *Genetic explanations cannot account for* ... patients who have no family history of the disorder.

Biochemical factors

Schizophrenia is caused by abnormal neurotransmitter levels.

Dopamine hypothesis Neurons fire too easily or too often, causing the characteristic symptoms of schizophrenia.

Evidence
- **Antipsychotic drugs** block dopamine receptors and reduce schizophrenic symptoms.
- **Parkinson's disease** The drug L-dopa, which raises levels of dopamine, causes schizophrenic-like symptoms in some people.

Limitations of biochemical explanation
- Excess dopamine can only explain *some* types of schizophrenia.
- Newer antipsychotics affect levels of other neurotransmitters, indicating that dopamine is not the only biochemical involved.
- *It cannot explain* why some schizophrenics have long periods of remission.

Brain dysfunction

Schizophrenics' brains have structural abnormalities.

Enlarged ventricles People who display negative symptoms are more likely to have enlarged ventricles in the brain and show greater cognitive disturbance.

Specific brain abnormalities Excess dopamine activity may be driven by a defect in the *prefrontal cortex* (Meyer-Lindenberg *et al.*, 2002).

Research support
Type II schizophrenics have less grey matter and smaller temporal and frontal lobes, *supporting the view that* ventricles are significant only in that they indicate reduced brain matter (Sigmundssen *et al.*, 2001).

This leads to the conclusion that ... Type I and Type II schizophrenia have different causes rather than 1 single biological cause.

However ... if schizophrenia were a function of brain dysfunction, then brain injury as a result of stroke or accident would lead to mental disorder, but this rarely happens.

Viral infection

Brain abnormalities associated with schizophrenia may be caused by exposure to viruses before birth.

Evidence
- Messias *et al.* (2001) found that mothers of schizophrenics were more likely to have been exposed to the influenza virus during pregnancy.

Strengths and weaknesses
- The viral hypothesis can explain patients with no family history of the disorder.
- There is no evidence that *all* schizophrenics have been exposed to viruses.

Probable questions

1. Critically consider **two or more** psychological explanations of schizophrenia. *(30 marks)*

2. (a) Outline **two** biological explanations of schizophrenia. *(15 marks)*

   (b) To what extent are the **two** biological explanations of schizophrenia outlined in part (a) supported by research evidence? *(15 marks)*

Possible questions

3. (a) Describe **one** biological explanation of schizophrenia. *(10 marks)*

   (b) Outline and evaluate evidence on which the explanation of schizophrenia you described in part (a) is based. *(20 marks)*

Chapter 8

Individual differences

Psychopathology >

Schizophrenia, depression, anxiety

Schizophrenia >

Depression

Anxiety disorders

Biological explanations of schizophrenia

Psychological explanations of schizophrenia

Psychological factors

Explanations are derived from the major psychological perspectives.

Psychodynamic explanations

Freud (1924) believed that schizophrenia was the result of:
- regression to a pre-ego stage
- attempts to re-establish ego control.

Behavioural explanations

Children who receive little social reinforcement for 'normal' behaviour later display inappropriate and bizarre behaviour.

Cognitive explanations

Further features of schizophrenia (e.g. delusional beliefs) appear as individuals attempt to make sense of the initial distorted sensory experiences of the disorder.

However ... there is a lack of evidence to support these claims, and other explanations exist to explain findings that might *appear* consistent with psychodynamic predictions.

Research support

Behavioural therapies (e.g. social skills training) have been successfully used with schizophrenic patients (Rodor *et al.*, 2002).

Physiological evidence

Meyer-Lindenberg *et al.* (2002) found a link between prefrontal cortex dysfunction, working memory and schizophrenia.

Sociocultural factors

These are explanations that stress the role of social and family relationships in this disorder.

Life events and schizophrenia

Discrete stressors (such as the death of a close relative) trigger schizophrenia.
- **Retrospective studies** Brown and Birley (1968) found that 50% of patients had experienced a major life event in the 3 weeks prior to a schizophrenic episode.
- **Prospective studies** Hirsch *et al.* (1996) found that life events made a significant *cumulative* contribution in the 12 months before a relapse.

Family relationships

- **Double bind theory** (Bateson *et al.*, 1956) Children who frequently receive contradictory messages from their parents are prevented from developing an internally coherent construction of reality.
- **High levels of expressed emotion** (e.g. criticism and emotional over-involvement) have been shown to influence relapse rate (e.g. Linszen *et al.*, 1997).

Social labelling

Scheff (1999) proposed that schizophrenics are *labelled* as mentally ill because they deviate from rules constructed by society.

The diathesis–stress model ... proposes that individuals may be genetically predisposed to become schizophrenic but the actual disorder depends on experience/stressors.

Norman and Malla (1993), in a review of research, **found little evidence that ...** schizophrenics have higher levels of stressors than the general population.

But they did find evidence of ... a relationship between stressors and the variation in severity of symptoms over time.

Supported by ... Berger (1965) who found that schizophrenic patients reported a higher number of double bind statements than a comparison group on non-schizophrenic patients.

Research on expressed emotion (EE) shows that patients who returned to homes with high EE were more likely to relapse than those returning to low EE homes, **thus confirming the importance of ...** psychological factors in schizophrenia.

However ... although EE explanations have received a great deal of research support, it is not clear whether high EE is a *cause* or an *effect* of schizophrenia.

However ... a focus on social labelling may draw attention away from the very disabling symptoms of schizophrenia, and the necessity of treatment.

Probable questions

1. Critically consider **two or more** psychological explanations of schizophrenia. *(30 marks)*

2. Outline and evaluate **one** psychological explanation of schizophrenia and **one** biological explanation of schizophrenia. *(30 marks)*

3. Critically consider **two or more** explanations of schizophrenia. *(30 marks)*

Possible questions

4. Describe and evaluate evidence on which **two or more** explanations of schizophrenia are based. *(30 marks)*

Chapter 8
Individual differences
Psychopathology >

Schizophrenia, depression, anxiety
Schizophrenia
Depression >
Anxiety disorders

Biological explanations of depression
Psychological explanations of depression

Genetic factors

Hammen (1997) suggests that as depression appears to run in families, genetic factors must be an important cause of the disorder.

Family studies
Harrington et al. (1993) found that 20% of first-degree relatives of depressives have depression, compared with 10% of non-relatives.

Twin studies
McGuffin et al. (1996) found a 46% concordance rate for identical twins and 20% for fraternal twins.

Adoption studies
Wender et al. (1986) found a higher incidence of depression in biological relatives of depressives, compared to a non-depressed control group.

Genes as diatheses
Genes create a predisposition for depression but must interact with environmental stressors to produce a depressive reaction.

Problems with genetic explanations
Concordance rates tend to be relatively low for depression, possibly because depression may be caused by genes that underlie different disorders, with the actual symptoms that develop being determined by environmental triggers.

Genes or environment?
Similarities among genetic relatives may be due to shared environments rather than simply shared genes.

Biochemical factors

The success of antidepressant medication is consistent with a biochemical process in depression.

Norepinephrine
Depression is thought to stem from a deficiency of the neurotransmitter norepinephrine in certain brain circuits.

Serotonin
The success of drugs that selectively block serotonin (SSRIs) suggests that low levels of serotonin at the synapse may be responsible for depression.

Cortisol hypersecretion
Overactivity in the HPA axis causes elevated levels of cortisol found in depressed patients.

It is difficult to establish cause and effect ... as depression may cause biochemical changes rather than the other way around.

The effects may be indirect ... since antidepressants reduce REM sleep: symptoms of depression are also reduced when depressives are deprived of REM sleep.

Supported by ... Mann et al. (1996), who found evidence of impaired serotonergic transmission in people with depression.

However ... it takes several weeks before antidepressants are effective, even though they raise neurotransmitter activity immediately.

This means that ... neurotransmitters cannot be the sole contributory cause of depression.

Brain dysfunction

Particular kinds of illness and injury may give rise to depression, suggesting that brain dysfunction may be a cause of the disorder.

Neurocognitive impairment
Porter et al. (2003) found pronounced neurocognitive impairment in depressives, suggesting an underlying brain dysfunction.

Neuroimaging studies
MRI scans have shown lower frontal lobe volume in depressives, which may act as a diathesis for depression.

Supported by ... Jacobs et al. (2000), who found that stress reduces neuron growth in the hippocampus and that the most effective antidepressant medications stimulate cell growth in this area.

Applications of this research include therapeutic benefits
If the specific areas of the brain that are responsible for depression can be identified, therapeutic intervention can be targeted on those areas.

Probable questions

1. Critically consider **two or more** biological explanations of depression. *(30 marks)*

2. (a) Outline **two** biological explanations of depression. *(15 marks)*

   (b) To what extent are the **two** biological explanations of depression outlined in part (a) supported by research evidence? *(15 marks)*

Possible questions

3. Compare and contrast biological and psychological explanations of depression. *(30 marks)*

Chapter 8

Individual differences

Psychopathology   >

Schizophrenia, depression, anxiety

Schizophrenia

Depression   >

Anxiety disorders

Biological explanations of depression

Psychological explanations of depression

Psychological factors

Explanations have been derived from the major psychological perspectives.

Psychodynamic explanations

• **Mourning and melancholia** Freud (1917) believed that depression was the result of prolonged mourning following the loss of a loved one, resulting in a permanent state of 'melancholia'.

• **Pathology of depression** Freud believed that depression is the result of anger (previously felt towards the lost person) turned against ourselves.

Cognitive explanations

• **Beck's (1967) theory of depression** Negative schemas and cognitive biases (e.g. overgeneralisation) maintain the *negative triad*, a pessimistic view of the self, the world and the future.

• **Learned helplessness** (Seligman, 1974) Depressed individuals acquire a sense of being unable to exercise control over their lives, and blame themselves for failure.

• **Hopelessness** The 'hopeless' person does not expect good things to happen in their life, does not believe he/she has the resources to cope with life's challenges, and so becomes depressed.

Research support

• There is some support for the role of early loss in later depression (e.g. Shah and Waller, 2000), although this association can be explained in terms of lack of parental care rather than loss of a parent.

• Loss explains only a small percentage of the cases of later depression.

Supported by ... Hammen and Krantz (1976) who showed that depressed individuals process and interpret information differently from their non-depressed counterparts.

However ... this does not indicate a causal relationship between negative thoughts and depression.

Which is supported by ... Segal and Ingram (1994) whose research suggests that negative thinking is a consequence of having depression rather than a causal factor.

Supported by ... Hiroto and Seligman (1974) who found that students exposed to uncontrollable aversive events were more likely to fail on cognitive tasks.

Therapeutic success

Unlike psychodynamic therapies, cognitive therapies are associated with successful treatment of depression **which supports the claim that** depression is largely a cognitive problem.

Cognitive explanations are able to explain gender differences in depression ... as a negative attributional style may be more common in women (Notmam and Nadelson, 1995).

Sociocultural factors

These are explanations that stress the role of life events and lack of social networks in the development of this disorder.

Life events and depression

• Depressed patients often experience higher numbers of negative life events in the year before a depressive episode. Vulnerability to these events is increased if other specific factors are also present.

• **Explaining the relationship** Life events may be the trigger in those with a genetic predisposition for depression, particularly those who have a depressive attributional style.

Interpersonal explanations

Depressed individuals tend to have sparse social networks and poor social skills.

Limitations of sociocultural explanations

• There is evidence that women rely more heavily on social support, and are therefore more likely to be adversely affected by its removal. This may not be as evident among males.

• Kessler (1997) claims that although research suggests that stressful life events can lead to episodes of depression, methodological problems with these studies compromise our ability to make clear causal inferences.

Evidence suggests ... that poor social skills (e.g. low social competence in primary age children) do play a causal role in the onset of depression (Cole, 1990).

Probable questions

1. Critically consider **two or more** psychological explanations of depression.   (30 marks)

2. Outline and evaluate **one** psychological explanation of depression and **one** biological explanation of depression.   (30 marks)

3. Critically consider **two or more** explanations of depression.   (30 marks)

Possible questions

4. Describe and evaluate evidence on which **two or more** explanations of depression are based.   (30 marks)

Chapter 8
Individual differences
Psychopathology   >

Schizophrenia, depression, anxiety
Schizophrenia
Depression
Anxiety disorders   >

Biological explanations of OCD
Psychological explanations of OCD

Genetic factors

A serotonin imbalance may be passed on from parents to children, suggesting that the tendency to develop OCD may be inherited.

Family and twin studies
Nestadt et al. (2000) found a strong familial link for OCD. A meta-analysis (Billett et al., 1998) found that identical twins were more likely than fraternal twins to develop OCD if the other twin had the disorder.

The COMT gene
A variation in the usual sequence of the COMT gene may contribute to OCD, particularly in men (Karayiorgou et al., 1997).

Because children and adults with OCD display different behaviours, **this suggests that ...** it is the general nature of this disorder that is inherited rather than the symptoms.

OCD may be linked to other disorders
OCD appears to be an expression of the same gene that determines Tourette's syndrome. Two-thirds of OCD patients also experience episodes of depression (Rasmussen and Eisen, 1992).

Research suggests that ... compared with other disorders, OCD has a relatively high concordance rate (e.g. Rasmussen and Tsuang, 1986).

However ... although there is evidence that OCD does have a genetic component, family and twin studies have found it difficult to disentangle the effects of genetics from those of a shared environment.

Biochemical factors

Research has found a link between low levels of serotonin and the development of OCD.

Serotonin
• People with OCD may have too little of the neurotransmitter serotonin for their nerve cells to communicate effectively.
• **Evidence from therapy** Drugs that increase the amount of serotonin in the brain (SSRIs) also reduce symptoms of OCD (Pigott et al., 1990).

Dopamine
High levels of dopamine may be involved in OCD, as antipsychotic drugs that block dopamine can reduce the symptoms of OCD.

However ... drug therapy may be insufficient or even unnecessary as behavioural therapy alone can reduce symptoms of OCD (Schwartz et al., 1996).
It is difficult to account for this finding ... if OCD has only biological causes.

Although ... low levels of serotonin may be a cause of OCD, this may simply be a consequence of the disorder.
Also ... we cannot rule out the possibility that SSRIs bring relief from OCD symptoms because they also alleviate the symptoms of depression that accompany OCD.

However ... although low levels of dopamine may cause malfunction of the basal ganglia, they may also be a consequence of its dysfunction (Haley et al., 2000).

Brain dysfunction

Certain areas of the brain appear to be affected by a serotonin imbalance, suggesting that brain dysfunction is a key factor in the onset of OCD.

Basal ganglia
• OCD may be caused by injury or degeneration of tissue linking the frontal cortex and basal ganglia.
• **Evidence from therapeutic intervention** OCD patients display increased glucose metabolism in the OFC–caudate nuclei loop, which can be reduced using SSRIs (Schwartz et al., 1996).

Support for the influence of brain dysfunction in OCD comes from ... the success of cingulotomies (in which a damaged part of the brain involved in OCD is removed) in reducing the symptoms of OCD (Dougherty et al., 2002).

Probable questions

1. Critically consider **two or more** biological explanations of any **one** anxiety disorder. (30 marks)

2. (a) Outline **two** biological explanations of any **one** anxiety disorder. (15 marks)

   (b) To what extent are the **two** biological explanations of the **one** anxiety disorder outlined in part (a) supported by research evidence? (15 marks)

Possible questions

3. (a) Describe **one** biological explanation of any **one** anxiety disorder. (10 marks)

   (b) Outline and evaluate evidence on which the explanation of the **one** anxiety disorder you described in part (a) is based. (20 marks)

Chapter 8
Individual differences
Psychopathology >

Schizophrenia, depression, anxiety
Schizophrenia
Depression
Anxiety disorders >

Biological explanations of OCD
Psychological explanations of OCD

Psychodynamic factors

Freud proposed that OCD arises when unacceptable wishes and impulses coming from the id are only partially repressed, thus creating anxiety.

Ego defence mechanisms
People with OCD use these to reduce the anxiety associated with unacceptable wishes and impulses. These include:
- **Isolation** (from unacceptable impulses)
- **Undoing** (through compulsive acts)
- **Reaction formation** (adopting opposite behaviours).

Regression OCD patients can avoid genital impulses by regressing to an earlier stage of development. Associated with this regression is the child-like belief that *thinking* about an event will make it happen, which in turn creates anxiety.

Research support
There is some evidence to support Freud's explanation of OCD (e.g. Apter *et al.*, 1997) and the basic underlying concepts of this explanation (Adams *et al.*, 1996).

However ... the use of psychoanalysis to treat OCD may have a *negative* effect on recovery (Salzman, 1980). If OCD is a product of unresolved conflicts, then therapy should help resolve these. The fact that it doesn't challenges this explanation.

Similarities with other theories
The Adlerian explanation (derived from Freud, suggesting OCD developed from a sense of inferiority) is similar to other perspectives, particularly humanistic ideas of mental illness (e.g. the view that low self-esteem blocks healthy growth – Rogers, 1959).

Behavioural factors

Thoughts become associated with a traumatic event (classical conditioning), and the resulting anxiety can be reduced by compulsive behaviours (operant conditioning).

Obsessions
Some people are conditioned early in life to regard certain thoughts as unclean or immoral; therefore these thoughts later create anxiety.

Compulsions
Compulsive rituals reduce the anxiety associated with obsessional thoughts, and so are reinforced.

Evidence
Based on research evidence, Rachman (1998) suggests that compulsive behaviours provide *quicker* relief from anxiety than would occur with spontaneous decay.

Supported by ... Rachman and Hodgson (1980) who found that compulsive behaviours provided quicker relief from anxiety than spontaneous decay alone (therefore are reinforcing).

Leads to behavioural therapy
The use of ERP therapy (where patients are exposed to situations that trigger their obsessions but are prohibited from engaging in compulsive behaviours) is effective for the majority of people (Albucher *et al.*, 1998).

Cognitive factors

People who are vulnerable to anxiety react to their obsessions and anxieties by developing maladaptive thought patterns.

Intrusive thoughts
In some people, intrusive thoughts are a cue for self-blame and the expectation that terrible things will happen. Depression weakens their ability to ignore such thoughts.

Neutralising anxiety
Individuals 'neutralise' obsessional thoughts by engaging in ritualistic compulsive behaviours. These become harder to resist because of the resultant reduction of anxiety.

Research support
People with OCD have more intrusive thoughts than normal (Clark, 1992) and report trying to do things that will neutralise these thoughts (Freeston *et al.*, 1992).

Cognitive therapies have been shown to be effective in treating OCD (e.g. Emmelkamp *et al.* 1988), **which supports the view that ...** OCD is a product of faulty thinking processes.

Probable questions

1. Critically consider **two or more** psychological explanations of any **one** anxiety disorder. *(30 marks)*
2. Outline and evaluate **one** psychological explanation of **one** anxiety disorder and **one** biological explanation of **one** anxiety disorder. *(30 marks)*
3. Critically consider **two or more** explanations of any **one** anxiety disorder. *(30 marks)*

Possible questions

4. Describe and evaluate evidence on which **two or more** explanations of any **one** anxiety disorder are based. *(30 marks)*

Chapter 9
Individual differences
Treating mental disorders >

Biological (somatic) therapies >
Behavioural therapies
Alternative therapies

Chemotherapy
ECT and psychosurgery

Antipsychotic drugs

These are drugs for treating psychotic illnesses such as schizophrenia and bipolar disorder .

When are they used? They help people with a serious psychosis function as well as possible and increase their subjective feelings of well-being.

How do they work?
- **Conventional antipsychotics** Dopamine antagonists reduce effects of *dopamine* and so reduce the symptoms of schizophrenia.
- **Atypical antipsychotics** additionally act on the *serotonin* system in the brain, and other systems involved in schizophrenia.

Research support
- Research (WHO, 2001) has shown that antipsychotics play an important role in the treatment of schizophrenia and can be effectively combined with psychotherapy.
- Atypical antipsychotics may ultimately be more effective as they have fewer side effects.

Antipsychotics may not always be appropriate because ... they do not always work, possibly because disorders such as depression and schizophrenia are not simply caused by biological factors.

Antidepressant drugs

Drugs such as the *tricyclics* and *SSRIs* relieve the symptoms of depression.

When are they used? These are used for depressive illnesses, and may be used to help symptoms of severe anxiety, OCD and eating disorders.

How do they work?
Antidepressants work by either reducing the rate of reuptake, or blocking enzymes that break down *serotonin* and *epinephrine*.
- **Tricyclics** block the reuptake mechanism that reabsorbs serotonin and epinephrine into the presynaptic cell.
- **SSRIs** selectively block the reuptake of serotonin into the presynaptic cell.

Placebo effects may explain effectiveness
Kirsch et al. (2002) found that people prescribed a placebo fared almost as well as those prescribed an antidepressant. *However ...* other studies (e.g. Mulrow *et al.*, 2000) found a stronger effect for the real drug.

Drugs do not offer a cure because ... they offer a temporary alleviation of symptoms rather than curing the underlying problem.

Side effects
All chemotherapies have side effects, often the reason why people stop taking their medication.

A problem with drug therapies is ... that they discourage patient responsibility, suggesting that the patient has no control over their recovery, which is achieved instead by external forces.

Tricyclics versus SSRIs
Newer SSRIs are more effective than tricyclics in severe depression, have fewer unwanted side effects and greater patient acceptance.

Anxiolytic drugs

These drugs are used to combat anxiety by bringing symptoms under control.

When are they used? They provide immediate symptom relief rather than prolonged treatment.

How do they work?
- **BZs** increase the action of GABA, which slows down the transmission of nerve signals in the brain.
- **Beta-blockers** block the action of epinephrine in the circulatory system, thus reducing the physical symptoms of anxiety.

Although ... BZs are the most effective and most quick-acting anxiolytics; even patients taking low doses experience withdrawal symptoms.

The efficacy ... of beta-blockers is limited to the short-term relief of physical symptoms.

Probable questions
1. Outline and evaluate **two or more** biological therapies. (30 marks)
2. (a) Outline **two** biological therapies. (15 marks)
   (b) Evaluate the **two** biological therapies you outlined in (a) with reference to issues surrounding their use (e.g. appropriateness and effectiveness). (15 marks)

Possible questions
3. (a) Describe chemotherapy as a form of biological therapy. (15 marks)
   (b) Evaluate the use of chemotherapy with reference to issues surrounding its use (e.g. appropriateness and effectiveness). (15 marks)
4. Discuss issues surrounding the use of biological therapies. (30 marks)

Chapter 9	Biological (somatic) therapies >	Chemotherapy
Individual differences	Behavioural therapies	ECT and psychosurgery
Treating mental disorders >	Alternative therapies	

ECT

In a nutshell – ECT is the application of an electric current to a patient's head which leads to a brain seizure, which in turn alleviates the symptoms of severe depression.

When is it used? ECT is generally used in severely depressed patients, particularly when the condition is considered to be potentially life-threatening.

How does it work?
- **Mechanism** An electric current is passed between two scalp electrodes to create a seizure lasting up to one minute.
- **Neurotransmitter function** ECT alters levels of receptors for serotonin and norepinephrine, increasing the quantities of these neurotransmitters in the synapse.
- **Neuroendocrine hypothesis** The ECT seizure is thought to cause a shift in the body's hormonal system, causing a decrease in the symptoms of depression.

Effectiveness
- Comer (2002) states that about two-thirds of patients improve after ECT treatment, but a high proportion relapse within 6 months.
- Some critics claim that equally high levels of improvement can be gained with placebo alone (Lowinger and Dobie, 1969).

Appropriateness
ECT is faster acting than drugs, and may be the only alternative if patients fail to respond to other treatments.

However ... there are side effects. These include *physical* side effects (e.g. impaired memory) and *psychological* side effects (e.g. fear and anxiety).

ECT may be unethical because ... a large proportion of those receiving ECT under the Mental Health Act have not consented to treatment.

There is a safer alternative (rTMS)
This involves passing high-intensity magnetic pulses through the skull. It is as effective as ECT with fewer side effects.

Psychosurgery

In a nutshell – Psychosurgery is surgical intervention to sever nerve fibres or destroy brain tissue, with the intent of modifying disturbances of behaviour with no known organic cause.

Stereotactic psychosurgery
When is it used? Computer-based stereotactic imaging is used as a precise way of surgically treating mental disorders that fail to respond to other forms of treatment.
How does it work? A sharp instrument is inserted into the brain and rotated to cut the white matter tracts to and from the prefrontal lobes.

Prefrontal lobotomy
When is it used? It is a surgical procedure involving the selective destruction of nerve fibres in the frontal lobe of the brain. It was performed on patients with severe affective disorders.
How does it work? It involves locating precise points within the brain and severing the connections. Examples include *cingulotomy* and *capsulotomy*.

Effectiveness
Cosgrove and Rauch (2001) reported that cingulotomies and capsulotomies are effective for between half and two-thirds of patients with OCD or depression.

Psychosurgery is inappropriate because ... Szasz (1978) claims that the psyche is not a part of the body, therefore it is impossible to perform surgery on it.

However ... there are potential side effects, e.g. irreversible damage to the brain may impair mental functioning.

Psychosurgery may be unethical because ... although informed consent is necessary prior to surgery, patients and their families may not be fully aware of the risks.

There is a safer alternative to psychosurgery
Deep brain stimulation uses a high-frequency current to interrupt the brain circuitry involved in OCD.

Probable questions
1. Outline and evaluate ECT **and** psychosurgery as biological therapies. (30 marks)
2. (a) Outline ECT **and** psychosurgery as biological therapies. (15 marks)

   (b) Evaluate ECT **and** psychosurgery with reference to issues surrounding their use (e.g. appropriateness and effectiveness). (15 marks)

Possible questions
3. (a) Describe ECT as a form of biological therapy. (15 marks)

   (b) Evaluate the use of ECT with reference to issues surrounding its use. (15 marks)
4. (a) Describe psychosurgery as a form of biological therapy. (15 marks)

   (b) Evaluate the use of psychosurgery with reference to issues surrounding its use (e.g. appropriateness and effectiveness). (15 marks)

Chapter 9
Individual differences
Treating mental disorders >
Biological (somatic) therapies
Behavioural therapies >
Alternative therapies
Classical conditioning therapies
Operant conditioning therapies

Aversion therapy

In a nutshell – Aversion therapy is a type of psychotherapy designed to cause patients to associate an undesirable behaviour with an aversive stimulus.

When is it used? Aversion therapy is used to suppress undesirable behaviours such as alcoholism and drug abuse.

How does it work?
- It is based on classical conditioning.
- Individuals are repeatedly presented with an aversive stimulus at the same time as they are engaging in an undesirable behaviour.
- The repeated association between the two leads to less desire to engage in the undesirable behaviour.

Covert sensitisation
This involves imagining aversive stimuli, e.g. repulsive scenes.

New developments
Some drugs used in the treatment of alcoholism not only associate nausea with alcohol but also reward abstinence (Badawy, 1999).

Effectiveness
- **Addictions** Some research has found no value in the use of aversion therapy in addictions, but others have (Smith *et al.*, 1997, with alcoholics and Smith, 1988, with smokers).
- **Homosexuality and sexual deviance** Bancroft and Marks (1968) found that half of males treated for sexual deviance were still 'improved' after 1 year. Attempts to evaluate effectiveness in the treatment of paedophilia are difficult as patients may 'fake' improvement to avoid further treatment.

Appropriateness
- **Patient dropout** Half of patients undergoing aversion therapy drop out, making evaluation of its effectiveness difficult.
- **Ethics** Aversion therapy can result in long-term psychological effects, including despair and depression, but these need to be balanced against the *benefits* of treatment.

Systematic desensitisation (SD)

In a nutshell – SD allows people to experience a feared object or situation gradually, whilst being in a state of relaxation.

When is it used? This treatment is particularly useful for treating psychological problems in which anxiety is the main difficulty.

How does it work?
- Patients gradually overcome their fears by learning to relax in the presence of (or by imagining) objects or images that would normally arouse anxiety.
- The therapist and patient construct a desensitisation hierarchy.
- The patient gradually works through each while relaxing (a relaxed state is incompatible with anxiety).

Effectiveness
Research has found that SD is successful for a range of anxiety disorders, including phobias (McGrath, 1990) and OCD (Albucher *et al.*, 1998).

Appropriateness of behavioural therapies
- These are generally quick and require less effort from the patient than other psychotherapies.
- *However ...* they are based on original work with non-human animals, but human anxiety may not always respond in the same way.

Psychoanalytic theorists claim behaviour therapies are inappropriate because ... treatment will simply result in a new symptom emerging if the underlying conflict is not resolved.
- *However ...* there is no evidence that this 'symptom substitution' does occur after SD or any other behavioural therapy.
- *However ...* although behaviour therapies target symptoms rather than the underlying problem, they do offer a cure in that they reduce problem behaviours.

Probable questions
1. Outline and evaluate **two or more** behavioural therapies. *(30 marks)*
2. (a) Outline **two** behavioural therapies based on classical conditioning. *(15 marks)*
   (b) Evaluate the **two** behavioural therapies based on classical conditioning outlined in (a) with reference to issues surrounding their use (e.g. appropriateness and effectiveness). *(15 marks)*

Possible questions
3. Discuss issues surrounding the use of behavioural therapies based on classical conditioning. *(30 marks)*

Chapter 9 | Biological (somatic) therapies | Classical conditioning therapies
Individual differences | Behavioural therapies > | **Operant conditioning therapies**
Treating mental disorders > | Alternative therapies

Behaviour modification

In a nutshell – If maladaptive behaviours are acquired through operant conditioning, it should be possible to *change* them using the same principles.

When is it used? It is used in a variety of educational and clinical settings, e.g. with learning difficulties and challenging behaviour.

How does it work?
- **ABC** A = antecedent event, B = changes in behaviour, C = consequences of behaviour.
- **Applied behaviour analysis (ABA)** ABA (Lovaas, 1987) is an intensive form of behaviour modification used with autistic children, that works by breaking autistic behaviour into separate behavioural problems that can be addressed individually.
- **Behaviour shaping** is reinforcement of successive approximations to a desired standard of performance, commonly used to help language development in young autistic children.

Effectiveness
- **Research support for ABA** Harris and Handleman (1994) reviewed several studies and found that 50% of autistic children were successfully integrated into mainstream classrooms after ABA.
- **Other applications** Formal versions of behaviour modification programmes have also been successfully used in business environments (Wertheim, 2003).
- **Reinforcement and punishment** Reinforcement has been shown to be more effective than punishment, as punishment only leads to short-term suppression of undesirable behaviour.

Behaviour modification is appropriate because ... these techniques have been widely applied with some success.

However ... they must be highly structured and started early to be really effective.

There are potential ethical problems
The CPA guidelines advise that such intrusive techniques should only be used after other less intrusive techniques have been tried.

Token economy

In a nutshell – This is a behaviour modification procedure in which patients are given tokens for desirable behaviour, that can be later 'traded' for desirable items and activities.

When is it used? It has been used to change negative symptoms of schizophrenia and in the management of classroom behaviour.

How does it work?
Six main steps:
1 Identify the target behaviour.
2 Identify the nature of the token.
3 Identify the unconditional reinforcers.
4 Determine the schedule of reinforcement.
5 Determine the exchange rate.
6 Determine the location and time of day for exchange.

Effectiveness
- **Schizophrenia** Token economies have been found to be very effective with schizophrenics (Allyon and Azrin, 1968; Paul and Lentz, 1977).
- **Other applications** Token economies have also been shown to be effective with violent patients (LePage, 1999) and with ADHD children (Lyon and Lagarde, 1997).

This technique may not always be appropriate
- Although it allows patients to improve their 'living skills', it may not offer a 'cure' for the underlying problem.
- Other simpler techniques may be just as effective and easier to execute.

There are potential ethical problems
US courts have ruled that withholding privileges and basic rights is not acceptable.

Probable questions

1. Outline and evaluate **two or more** behavioural therapies based on operant conditioning. *(30 marks)*

2. (a) Outline **two** behavioural therapies based on operant conditioning. *(15 marks)*

   (b) Evaluate the **two** behavioural therapies based on operant conditioning outlined in (a) with reference to issues surrounding their use (e.g. appropriateness and effectiveness). *(15 marks)*

3. Compare and contrast biological and behavioural therapies. *(30 marks)*

Possible questions

4. Discuss issues surrounding the use of behavioural therapies based on operant conditioning. *(30 marks)*

Chapter 9

Individual differences

Treating mental disorders >

Biological (somatic) therapies

Behavioural therapies

Alternative therapies >

Psychodynamic therapies

Cognitive–behavioural therapies

Psychoanalysis

In a nutshell – The focus of psychoanalysis is the removal of underlying conflicts the person has repressed into their unconscious mind.

When is it used? Psychoanalysis aims to bring unconscious conflicts into the conscious mind, where they can more easily be dealt with. It is mostly used in the treatment of disorders such as obsessional behaviour and phobias, rather than psychotic disorders.

How does it work?

- **Repression** Thoughts and memories that might create anxiety are excluded from the conscious mind, and revealed during therapy.

- **Free association** The patient expresses thoughts as they occur, and the therapist helps him/her to interpret these thoughts.

- **Therapist interpretation** The therapist interprets free associations and dream content. The patient may resist these interpretations or display transference towards the therapist.

- **Working through** The patient and client revisit issues time and again over an extended period, in order to gain greater clarity of the problem.

Effectiveness

Freud used the successful outcomes of his own patients as proof that psychoanalysis worked.
However … critics have claimed that the evidence for these patients actually being 'cured' is debatable (Guttman, 2001).

Psychoanalysis is less effective than other therapies

- Eysenck (1965) claimed that psychoanalysis was far less effective than eclectic (mixed) therapies.

- Smith *et al.* (1980) found that psychoanalysis was not as effective as cognitive–behavioural therapy, and almost equal to a placebo group.

Appropriateness

Freud introduced the notion that mental illness might have a psychological cause and therefore could be treated by psychoanalysis.

Limitations of psychoanalysis

- It is based on a non-falsifiable theory.

- There is little evidence to support the claim that repressed memories are recalled accurately.

As a result of these limitations … modern psychoanalysis has moved away from Freud's ideas, with a more dynamic focus on just one problem.

Play therapy

In a nutshell – Play therapy is a development of psychodynamic principles used exclusively for young children.

When is it used? Play therapy is mostly used with children between the ages of 3 and 11, with a wide range of emotional problems, including issues surrounding abuse.

How does it work?

- **Non-directive play therapy** Children create play situations that resemble the emotional problem they cannot verbalise. The therapist observes and notes the symbolic actions of the play.

- **Directive play therapy** The therapist takes a more active role and structures the session for diagnostic and assessment purposes.

Effectiveness

- **Non-directive play therapy** has been shown to be effective in a range of contexts, including child witnesses of domestic violence (Kot *et al.*, 1999).

- **Directive play therapy** This is particularly effective when used in a school setting; effectiveness is increased when used in conjunction with non-directive play therapy.

Appropriateness

Play therapy remains one of the few techniques suitable for working with children.
However … a lack of a rigorous methodology means this technique is often loosely applied.

There are potential ethical problems … since ethical guidelines for therapeutic conduct do not relate well to play therapy; therefore more specialised guidelines should be developed.

Probable questions [see page 69 for further questions]

1. (a) Outline **two** therapies derived from either the psychodynamic or cognitive–behavioural models of abnormality. *(15 marks)*

   (b) Evaluate the **two** therapies derived from either the psychodynamic or cognitive–behavioural models of abnormality outlined in (a) with reference to issues surrounding their use (e.g. appropriateness and effectiveness). *(15 marks)*

Possible questions

2. Compare and contrast biological therapies and therapies derived from either the psychodynamic or cognitive–behavioural models of abnormality. *(30 marks)*

Chapter 9
Individual differences
Treating mental disorders >

Biological (somatic) therapies
Behavioural therapies
Alternative therapies >

Psychodynamic therapies
Cognitive–behavioural therapies

Rational–emotive behavioural therapy (REBT)

In a nutshell – REBT is based on the idea that many problems are the result of faulty or irrational thinking.

When is it used? REBT helps clients to understand the nature and consequences of their irrational thinking, and helps them to substitute more effective problem-solving methods.

How does it work?
- **ABC model** A – activating events, B – beliefs, C – consequences.
- **Irrational beliefs** are experienced as self-defeating thoughts, and lead to unproductive outcomes. Changing these leads to more productive outcomes.
- **Disputing** The patient is encouraged to dispute self-defeating thoughts through: logical disputing, empirical disputing, pragmatic disputing.

Effectiveness
- Ellis (1957) claimed a 90% success rate for REBT.
- A meta-analysis of psychotherapies cited REBT as having the second highest success rate of the 10 therapies reviewed (Smith and Glass, 1977).

Problems with evaluating effectiveness
- Many of the participants are of the YAVIS type, i.e. young, attractive, verbal, etc. (thus limiting *generalisability*).
- Meta-analyses do not take account of the *consistency* with which a particular method (REBT) has been applied by different therapists.

Appropriateness
REBT is useful for both clinical and non-clinical groups.
However ... although irrational beliefs may be maladaptive, there is evidence that they are frequently more realistic (Alloy and Abrahmson, 1979).

There are potential ethical problems
REBT is considered one of the more aggressive and judgmental therapies, which raises ethical concerns about the degree of manipulation by the therapist.

Stress inoculation training (SIT)

In a nutshell – SIT is a form of cognitive therapy which helps individuals develop a coping strategy before a stressful situation arises.

When is it used? This has been used in a variety of stress-related situations including anger management and avoidance behaviour in rape victims.

How does it work?
1 **Conceptualisation** The client is taught to view stressors as specific problems that can be solved.
2 **Skills acquisition** Cognitive and behavioural skills are taught and practiced.
3 **Application** Clients are given the opportunity to apply these skills in situations that become increasingly stressful.

SIT has been shown to be effective in ...
- the treatment of ophidiophobia (Meichenbaum, 1977)
- stress reduction in college students (Fontana *et al.*, 1999)
- a wide range of stress-related problems, including anger reduction in people with post-traumatic stress (Chemtob *et al.*, 1997).

SIT may not always be appropriate because ...
- the nature of SIT makes it a lengthy and unnecessarily complex technique
- it is possible that a simpler procedure would have the same effectiveness.

There are fewer ethical problems because ... SIT is more client-centred than REBT, and so gives more choice to the client, and less to the therapist.

CBTs appear less suitable ... for long-term and severe disorders (James and Blackburn, 1995).

Probable questions [see page 68 for further questions]

1. Outline and evaluate **two or more** therapies derived from either the psychodynamic or cognitive–behavioural models of abnormality. *(30 marks)*

Possible questions

2. Discuss issues surrounding the use of therapies derived from either the psychodynamic or cognitive–behavioural models of abnormality. *(30 marks)*

Chapter 10	Issues	>	Gender bias
Perspectives	Debates		Cultural bias
Issues and debates	>		Ethical issues
			The use of non-human animals

In psychological theories

Major theories are frequently characterised by a gender bias resulting from a 'male as norm' perspective.

Types of gender bias (Hare-Mustin and Maracek, 1990)
- **Alpha-bias** assumes real and enduring differences between men and women.
- **Beta-bias** ignores or minimises differences between men and women.

Alpha-biased theories
- **Freud** represented women as inferior because they were jealous of men's penises and didn't undergo the same Oedipus conflict.
- **Gilligan** (1982) proposed that men and women reason differently about moral issues. Girls develop a morality of care whereas men have a preoccupation with justice.

Beta-biased theories
- **Kohlberg** produced a stage theory of moral reasoning which he claimed represented males *and* females using a set of dilemmas based on abstract principles.
- **Fight or flight** is usually represented as a universal response, but among our ancestors, a greater biological investment in offspring among females may have led to a different response to stress.

However
- Critics such as Horney (1926) claim that men may also envy women's ability to have children ('womb envy').
- Bruehl (1990) argues that Freud's view of women simply reflected the patriarchal structure of his time, and therefore might be expected.

Lack of research support
- This view of gender differences tends not to be supported by research.
- Also, in emphasising differences between men and women, it minimises differences *between* women.

A consequence of this is that … women are portrayed as morally inferior; a product, according to Kohlberg, of a life lived mainly in the home.

This distinction is supported by … Taylor *et al.* (2000), who have provided evidence to support the evolution of a 'tend and befriend' response to stress in human females.

In psychological studies

Traditional research methods in psychology have been biased towards males.

Androcentrism
Human behaviour tends to be described *by* males from a male perspective.
- **Media effects research** has tended to focus on male-on-male physical violence, and on its effects on male viewers.
- **PMS research** provides a biological account of women's behaviour and emotional states that represents them as 'prisoners of their own biology'.

Gender bias
- **Researcher bias** may be evident in a marginalisation of female research interests. Males may propose hypotheses that promote stereotypical differences between men and women.
- **Methodological bias** may be evident in biased sampling or the use of methods (e.g. laboratory experiments) that disadvantage women.

Support for this view
- Paik and Comstock (1994), who showed that only 2% of research focuses solely on females.
- Other research has shown that in many 'slasher' films *women* are the main aggressors (Cowan and O'Brien, 1990).

The validity of this research is compromised by … a lack of agreement over PMS symptoms.

A consequence of this research is that … it is used to justify occupational discrimination against women.

An alternative approach comes from … feminist psychology, which aims to increase awareness of and to compensate for gender bias in research.

Probable questions

1. Discuss gender bias in psychological research (theories **and/or** studies). *(30 marks)*

2. (a) Outline **two** types of gender bias in psychology. *(5 marks)*

   (b) Discuss gender bias in psychological research (theories **and/or** studies). *(25 marks)*

3. 'Psychology has represented male behaviour as the norm, and consequently has ignored female behaviour and experience.'

   Discuss gender bias in **two or more** psychological theories, with reference to issues such as those raised in the quotation above. *(30 marks)*

Possible questions

4. Discuss gender bias in **two** psychological theories. *(30 marks)*

Chapter 10	Issues	>	Gender bias
Perspectives	Debates		**Cultural bias**
Issues and debates	>		Ethical issues
			The use of non-human animals

In psychological theories

Traditional psychology is characterised by a theoretical bias reflecting US and European culture alone.

Types of cultural bias
- **Ethnocentrism** is an emphasis on one's own ethnic or cultural group as a basis for judgments about other groups.
- **Eurocentrism** is an emphasis on European (or Western) theories, assuming they are superior.

Economic theories of relationships
These may only apply to individualist cultures (Moghaddam, 1998).

Kohlberg's theory of moral understanding
This may be ideologically biased toward Western cultures. If used to compare cultures this may lead to invalid conclusions.

Neuropsychology
This may lack universal validity. It is possible that brain organisation may reflect the very different ecological demands made on members of different cultures.

Responses to cultural bias
Psychology has responded to claims of cultural bias through the development of *indigenous psychologies* and through *afrocentrism* as a reaction to the eurocentric bias which devalues non-European peoples.

Research evidence challenges the claim that ... individualist and collectivist cultures differ in the ways suggested by Moghaddam (Takano and Osaka, 1999). The apparent individualist–collectivist distinction may be a product of the *fundamental attribution error* (overestimating the influence of personal characteristics and underestimating the influence of situational factors).

Are cross-cultural comparisons valid?
Yes Post-conventional reasoning tends to be absent from traditional village societies (Snarey, 1985).
No Other, equally mature, forms of moral reasoning may be operating.

Research has supported the importance of ... the cultural environment in shaping the organisation of the human nervous system (e.g. Ardila, 1995).

In psychological studies

Researchers and participants have tended to come from either Europe or the US.

The emic–etic distinction
- **Emic approaches** study behaviour from within a culture, study only that culture, and produce findings significant only within that culture.
- **Etic approaches** study behaviour from outside a culture, study many cultures, and produce findings considered to have universal applications.

Obedience studies
Although replications of Milgram's obedience study have been carried out in different cultures, methodological differences makes it difficult to draw meaningful conclusions across cultures.

Psychopathology
Researchers may impose their own culture's mental illness categories onto behaviour that is normal elsewhere. *Cultural relativism* stresses the importance of considering the unique aspects of each culture when determining what is abnormal.

Difficulties with direct comparisons in cross-cultural research
- Difficulties of translation
- The meaning of variables under study in different cultures
- Differences in participants (e.g. the nature of student populations in different cultures)
- Cultural differences in the research tradition, which influence how people respond during research

A consequence of cultural bias is ... that if cultural factors are ignored in research on psychopathology, then inappropriate conclusions may be drawn.

This has implications for ... the treatment (or non-treatment) of psychopathological behaviour in those cultures.

Probable questions
1. Discuss cultural bias in psychological research (theories **and/or** studies). *(30 marks)*
2. (a) Outline **two** types of cultural bias in psychology. *(5 marks)*
   (b) Discuss cultural bias in psychological research (theories **and/or** studies). *(25 marks)*
3. 'Psychological research is focused almost exclusively on Western cultures. This invalidates any claim that we may have a universal understanding of human behaviour.'
   Discuss cultural bias in **two or more** theories of psychology, with reference to issues such as those raised in the quotation above. *(30 marks)*

Possible questions
4. Discuss cultural bias in **two** psychological theories. *(30 marks)*

Chapter 10	Issues	>	Gender bias
Perspectives	Debates		Cultural bias
Issues and debates	>		**Ethical issues**
			The use of non-human animals

In psychological investigations

An ethical issue is a dilemma that psychologists might face in their research.

Deception
Researchers may be guilty of deliberately misleading a participant (*active* deception) or withholding important information from them.

Informed consent
Some research designs (e.g. those that use implicit coercion) may compromise the participants' ability to consent freely.

Right to withdraw
It is the right of each participant to decline to disclose sensitive information and to withdraw at any time.

Consequences of deception in research
- It may make participants suspicious about a research investigation.
- It removes the ability of participants to give fully *informed* consent.

However ... despite this, research suggests people do not object to the use of deception in research (Christiansen, 1988).

An implication of this is that ... a lack of secretive practices is more likely to gain public respect.

Problems surrounding informed consent are more widespread because ... recent developments in Internet-based research have posed new difficulties in ensuring that participants give their *informed* consent.

However ... some researchers appear to operate as if the right to withdraw operates only until the end of a participant's role in a study, rather than allowing them the opportunity to withdraw their data later on.

Socially sensitive research

In a nutshell – Studies that have potential social consequences either for the participants themselves, or the class of individuals they represent, for example, studies on IQ and race (Scarr and Weinberg, 1983).

The nature of socially sensitive research
- **Asking the right questions** Sometimes even just posing a particular research question may be seen as adding scientific credibility to the prevailing prejudice.
- **Misuse of research findings** Some research findings on interracial differences can be used to support divisive and discriminatory social policies.

Ethical issues in socially sensitive research include:
- Privacy
- Confidentiality
- Poor methodology
- Equitable treatment
- Ownership of data

Wider impact of research
It may not be sufficient to safeguard the interests of research participants: the probable impact on the larger social group should also be considered.

Disadvantaging marginalised groups
Some groups may be excluded from research (and any positive consequences that might arise from such research) or misrepresented when they *have* been included.

However ... researchers also have social responsibilities, so ignoring important but sensitive areas of research would amount to an abdication of the social responsibilities of the researcher.

Inadequacy of ethical guidelines
Ethical guidelines do not deal with all possible ways that research can harm a section of society (e.g. through inappropriate interpretations of findings).

A consequence of socially sensitive research is that ... it may offer scientific credibility to abuse and discriminate against some groups in society.

Probable questions
1. With reference to **two or more** psychological investigations, discuss ethical issues in research with human participants. *(30 marks)*
2. Discuss the ethics of socially sensitive research. *(30 marks)*

Possible questions
3. (a) Outline **two or more** ethical issues involved in psychological investigations using human participants. *(15 marks)*

   (b) To what extent does socially sensitive research pose special ethical problems for the researcher? *(15 marks)*

4. 'The rights of research participants to be treated openly, honestly and with dignity, must take precedence over all other aspects of the research process.'

   With reference to issues such as those in the quotation above, discuss ethical issues in psychological investigations using human participants. *(30 marks)*

Chapter 10	Issues	>	Gender bias
Perspectives	Debates		Cultural bias
Issues and debates	>		Ethical issues
			The use of non-human animals

Constraints on the use of animals

These include *legal* constraints (Animals Act, 1986) and *ethical* constraints (e.g. BPS guidelines).

Legal
Animal research in the UK is legislated by the Animals Act (1986) which issues licences and is enforced by inspectors.

Ethical
BPS guidelines consider, for example:

- Ethical considerations
- Numbers of animals
- Motivation through deprivation

Alternatives to animal research: the '3 Rs'
This was first published by Russell and Burch (1959). A recent House of Lords report (2002) emphasises commitment to the '3 Rs':

- **Reduction** of the number of animals used to obtain information (e.g. using improved experimental designs)
- **Replacement** of animals by alternative methods (e.g. brain scanning and imaging)
- **Refinement** using procedures that minimise stress and enhance animal well-being, which has the additional benefit of ensuring that animals behave more 'naturally'.

Arguments *for* the use of animals

Arguments *for* animal research also have counterarguments (on the right) that challenge their assumptions and conclusions.

Scientific arguments
- Animal research has been the major contributor to our understanding of basic learning processes.
- Animal research has contributed significantly to our understanding of drug abuse and dependence.
- The basic physiology of the brain and nervous systems of all mammals is the same.

Moral arguments
- Because of the important contribution of animal research, it would be morally wrong *not* to use animals in research.
- Human life has greater intrinsic value than animal life, based on rights and responsibilities.
- Less invasive procedures have been developed which minimise animal suffering.
- Animal research is controlled by strict laws (Use of Animals Act) and codes of conduct (e.g. BPS).

Arguments *against* the use of animals

Scientific arguments
- 'Science at any cost' involves the mindset that scientific knowledge justifies harming innocent individuals. This endangers all who are vulnerable, not just animals.
- Critics argue that animal studies can neither confirm nor refute hypotheses about human behaviour.
- Surveys of the value of animal research suggest that in clinical psychology this may have been overstated (Shapiro, 1998).

Moral arguments
- These have been accomplished at considerable expense in terms of animal suffering.
- Animals have an 'inherent value' including a right to be treated with respect and not harmed.
- If researchers were not allowed to use animals in research, they would be forced to develop alternatives.
- Ethical guidelines are based mainly on costs and benefits, which ignore the substantive rights of animals in favour of humans.

Ethical arguments
- **Singer's utilitarian view** What is ethically acceptable is what brings the greatest pleasure and happiness to the greatest number, yet does not put the interests of one species over another's (*speciesism*).
- **Regan's animal's rights argument** All animals have rights based on their 'inherent value' rather than being treated as 'renewable resources' (violation of the principle of respect).

Probable questions
1. Discuss the use of non-human animals in psychological research. (30 marks)
2. Discuss arguments (both ethical **and** scientific) **for** the use of non-human animals in psychological investigations. (30 marks)
3. Discuss arguments **against** the use of non-human animals in psychological investigations. (30 marks)

Possible questions
4. Critically consider constraints on the use of non-human animals in psychological investigations. (30 marks)
5. 'Psychologists have a special responsibility to protect the rights and welfare of non-human animals in research.'

With reference to the issues in the quotation above, discuss the use of non-human animals in psychological research. (30 marks)

Chapter 10	Issues	**Free will and determinism**
Perspectives	Debates >	Reductionism
Issues and debates >		Psychology as science
		Nature–nurture

Free will in psychological research

Individuals are seen as capable of self-determination.
Rogers' self theory (1959) suggested that only when an individual takes self-responsibility is personal growth possible, resulting in psychological health.
Maslow's hierarchy of needs People have an innate tendency to move towards *autonomy* (self-determination) and *self-actualisation*.

Research support for free will ... can be seen in the role of control in stress. Kim *et al.* (1997) found that children who felt in control showed less evidence of stress during parental divorce.

Arguments *for* free will

- **Subjective experience** Most people *believe* they have free will.
- People are **self-determining**, do make decisions and are free to follow their desires and inclinations.
- The basis of **moral responsibility** is that individuals are responsible for their own actions, i.e. can exercise free will.

Arguments *against* free will

A subjective sense of free will isn't the same ... as *proof*.

People may not be self-determining because ... the *illusion* of free will does not confirm the *existence* of free will. In addition, self-determination may be appropriate only in *individualist* cultures, where autonomy and independence are encouraged.

Most psychological theories of moral development ... (Kohlberg) present moral thinking and behaviour as being *determined* by internal and/or external forces.

Reconciling free will and determinism

Valentine (1992) suggests that behaviour that is highly constrained appears involuntary, whereas less constrained behaviour *appears* voluntary.
This is supported by ... a study showing people felt they had more free will when in situations with little responsibility (Westcott, 1982).

Determinism in psychological research

An individual's behaviour is shaped or controlled by internal or external forces.
Learning theory
- **Attachment** is explained in terms of conditioning.
- **Relationships** We are attracted to people whom we associate with rewards (reinforcement-affect theory).
Psychoanalytic theory
- **Personality** is a mixture of innate drives and early experience.
- **Dreams** are determined by unfulfilled wishes.

However ... attachment is not determined through an association with feeding (Harlow, 1959).
There is some support for ... reinforcement-affect theory (Griffit and Guay, 1969).

Freud's theory of personality **has little empirical support**.
The same is true for his theory of dreams although there is some supporting evidence (e.g. Solms, 2000).

Arguments *for* determinism

- **There is increasing evidence of genetic influences** on behaviour.
- A belief in **causal relationships** between events is the basis of scientific research.
- **Free will can be explained in a determinist framework,** as another aspect of behaviour that is *determined* by brain activity.

Arguments *against* determinism

It is doubtful that ... total genetic determination will ever be found for any behaviour.

Even within the physical sciences ... it is now accepted that there is no such thing as total determinism (Dennett, 2003).

Determinist explanations oversimplify ... human behaviour, which is influenced by many factors.

Probable questions

1. Discuss the free will versus determinism debate with reference to **two or more** psychological theories. *(30 marks)*

2. (a) Explain what is meant by the terms 'free will' and 'determinism'. *(5 marks)*

   (b) With reference to **two or more** psychological theories, discuss the free will versus determinism debate. *(25 marks)*

Possible questions

3. Critically consider arguments for determinism in psychology. *(30 marks)*

Chapter 10	Issues	Free will and determinism
Perspectives	Debates >	**Reductionism**
Issues and debates >		Psychology as science
		Nature–nurture

Reductionism

Reductionism involves breaking down a complex phenomenon into simpler components.

Kinds of reductionism (Rose, 1997)
- Reductionism as methodology (experimental reductionism)
- Reductionism as an explanation
- Reductionism as a philosophy

However ... experimental reductionism in research can produce valuable results (e.g. in research on EWT).

➤ **But such research may be misleading ...** particularly given the need to *operationalise* variables to make them measurable.

Examples in psychological research

Reductionism is evident, albeit in different forms, in many different areas of psychology.

Physiological reductionism
This involves the reduction of (e.g. mental illness) to the action of neurotransmitters, hormones, etc.

Environmental reductionism
Behaviourist explanations propose that all behaviour can be reduced to a simple relationship between the behaviour and events in the environment.

Evolutionary reductionism
All behaviour can be explained in terms of natural and sexual selection. This presumes that behaviour can be reduced to genetic influences and the principle of adaptiveness.

Machine reductionism
Cognitive psychology frequently makes use of information processing analogies (e.g. the multi-store model), representing human cognition as 'machine-like'.

The value of such research is highlighted by ... the use of drugs in the treatment of mental disorders which has reduced the numbers in institutions, but the success rate of such treatments is variable.

However ... behaviourist explanations were developed as a result of work with non-human animals, which may ignore other influences on behaviour, including cognitive and emotional factors.

Although ... evolutionary explanations may distract us from other possible explanations, *they help us to make sense of* behaviours because they focus on adaptiveness or function (i.e. the *ultimate* rather than *proximate* function).

Recent developments ... represent mental functions as connectionist networks, which are considered *holist* because the network as a whole behaves differently from the individual parts.

Arguments *for* reductionism

All animals are made of atoms
This leads to two assumptions:
- Behaviour is simply the sum of its parts.
- Every physical event has a physical cause.

Reduction is productive
It helps us to understand how things work, e.g. how the experience of stress is linked to actions of the nervous system.
Behaviour can be investigated on *various levels*, all of which contribute to our overall understanding of that behaviour.

Arguments *against* reductionism

Contradictory evidence
Depressed patients who received *psychotherapy* experienced the same changes in serotonin levels in the brain as those receiving drugs (Martin et al., 2001).

Experimental research does not always ... equate to real life and may dangerously misrepresent it.

If low levels of explanation are taken in isolation ... we may miss the *meaning* of a behaviour, or be distracted from other possible explanations for the same behaviour.

Probable questions

1. 'By adopting a reductionist approach, we are in danger of overlooking the real causes of human behaviour.'

   With reference to issues such as those in the quotation above, discuss the value of a reductionist approach to psychological theory **and/or** research. *(30 marks)*

2. (a) Explain what is meant by 'reductionism' in psychology. *(5 marks)*

   (b) With reference to **two or more** areas of psychology, discuss different examples of reductionism. *(25 marks)*

Possible questions

3. Describe and evaluate arguments **for** reductionist explanations in psychology. *(30 marks)*

4. Describe and evaluate arguments **against** reductionist explanations in psychology. *(30 marks)*

Chapter 10	Issues	>	Free will and determinism
Perspectives	Debates	>	Reductionism
Issues and debates	>		**Psychology as science**
			Nature–nurture

Definitions and varieties of science

Definition of science A branch of knowledge conducted on objective principles involving the systematic observation of, and experiment with, phenomena.

Varieties
- **Hard and soft science** Physics and chemistry are regarded as hard sciences, psychology and sociology as soft, less rigorous sciences.
- **Induction and deduction** Induction involves reasoning from the particular to the general, deduction from the general to the particular. This is reflected in the *hypothetico–deductive* model in psychology.

Social sciences do use the scientific method ... and therefore may be considered *scientific*.

However ... Kitzinger (1987) claims the notion of objective science is a myth, especially in psychology.

Criticisms of the inductive approach
Logical positivism concerns description rather than explanation, but resulted in natural laws which could not be disproved.

Criticisms of the deductive approach
Falsifiability is an alternative to logical positivism, but was criticised by Kuhn (1962) who claimed that theories are *not* fine-tuned by a successive series of experiments.

Arguments *for* psychology as a science

Desirable
Scientific psychology offers verifiable knowledge rather than commonsense explanations of behaviour.

Goals of science
Psychologists generate models that can be falsified and conduct well controlled experiments to test these models.

Some levels are scientific
Lower levels of analysis (e.g. physiological) may be considered *hard* science and higher levels (e.g. social psychological) *soft* science.

Supporting argument
Human behaviour is ultimately caused, therefore the same achievements are possible in psychology as in the physical sciences.

Although ... an APA report (Koch, 1992) concluded that psychological research has resulted in verifiable descriptions of behaviour.

It also concluded that ... the explanations derived from these descriptions are more opinion than fact.

However ... using scientific methods doesn't make psychology a science; maybe it is a 'pseudo-science' (Miller, 1983).

However ... many of the lower levels of psychology actually belong to other disciplines (e.g. physiology), thus detracting from psychology's status as a science in its own right.

Arguments *against* psychology as a science

No single paradigm
A science has a unified set of assumptions and methods. Psychology, therefore, might be considered 'pre-' science.

Lack external validity
Findings from experiments are not always supported by real-life observations (e.g. Mandel's analysis of Milgram's obedience research).

Lack internal validity
Psychological research is fraught with threats to internal validity (e.g. demand characteristics).

Goals not appropriate
Laing (1965) felt that it was wrong to see schizophrenia as a complex physical system that has gone wrong.

However ... there *are* a number of 'mini' paradigms coexisting in psychology, each with its own set of explanations and methods.

However ... there are some success stories, such as the application of laboratory-derived knowledge to explain bystander behaviour.

However ... such problems also occur in the physical sciences (e.g. the uncertainty principle).

However ... most of the recent advances in our understanding (and therefore treatment) of schizophrenia have been achieved using scientific research within the medical model.

Probable questions
1. Critically consider the view that psychology is a science. *(30 marks)*
2. (a) Outline what is meant by 'science' in the context of psychological research. *(5 marks)*
   (b) Outline and evaluate arguments **for** the claim that psychology is a science. *(25 marks)*

Possible questions
3. Critically consider arguments **for** the claim that psychology is a science. *(30 marks)*
4. Critically consider arguments **against** the claim that psychology is a science. *(30 marks)*

Chapter 10	Issues	Free will and determinism
Perspectives		Reductionism
Issues and debates >	Debates >	Psychology as science
		Nature–nurture

Definitions

Nature This refers not just to abilities present at birth, but any ability determined by genes. Early psychologists were influenced by Darwinism and the idea of *innate tendencies*.
Nurture Everything is learned through experience. We are born like a '*blank slate*' (Locke), a view taken by the *behaviourists*.

However ... it is not always possible to disentangle nature and nurture, for example *transgenerational effects*, which are apparently inherited effects that skip a generation.

Assumptions in psychological research

Nature
- **Evolutionary psychologists** assume that behaviour is a product of *natural selection*.
- **Physiological psychologists** assume that there are genetically programmed systems.

Nurture
- **Radical behaviourists** (such as Skinner) assume that all behaviour can be explained in terms of experience alone.
- **Non-behaviourist explanations** assume that experience is important, e.g. double bind theory of schizophrenia (Bateson *et al.*, 1956).

The nature–nurture debate
- **Perception** The debate is between direct theories (i.e. nature) and constructivist theories (i.e. nurture).
- **Intelligence** A large component of variation in IQ is caused by genetic factors, but there is equally strong evidence for the influence of nurture.
- **Mental illness** Both biological and psychological explanations have been proposed and supported by empirical evidence.

However ... a purely genetic or adaptive argument cannot explain vast amounts of evidence showing how experience alters the path of development.

Evolutionary theories have been criticised as ... speculative, because there is little hard evidence to support them.

However ... there are limitations to the influence of experience as conditioning is also affected by innate factors, e.g. *biological preparedness*.

Neither theory can explain ... all aspects of visual perception, e.g. Blakemore and Cooper (1970) showed how kittens deprived of experience (*nurture*) later showed compensatory changes in the brain (*nature*).

Environmental influences are minimised in ... supportive and affluent families, which maximises the influence of genes.

However ... a poor environment allows environment to have a larger influence.

Research support
Turkheimer *et al.* (2003) found that most of the variability in IQ of children from poor backgrounds was accounted for by their shared environment.

The diathesis–stress model represents both nature *and* nurture in the development of a mental disorder.

Different views regarding the relationship

Nature affects nurture
Genetic factors:
- create an individual's *microenvironment* (reactive effect)
- create a passive influence through parental behaviour
- cause children to actively select certain experiences.

Nurture affects nature
The brain may be changed as a result of experience (*neural plasticity*).

Ridley (2003) refers to *nature exerting its influence via nurture* (e.g. the influence of the gene *RSG4* in schizophrenics is modified by experience).

Most behaviour is *best explained by* a combination of nature and nurture, e.g. perception, intelligence, mental illness.

Probable questions

1. Discuss the nature–nurture debate with reference to **two or more** psychological theories and/or studies. *(30 marks)*

2. (a) Explain what is meant by the terms 'nature' and 'nurture'. *(5 marks)*

   (b) With reference to **two or more** psychological theories, discuss assumptions made about nature and nurture. *(25 marks)*

Possible questions

3. Discuss different views regarding the relationship between nature and nurture. *(30 marks)*

Chapter 11
Perspectives
Approaches >

The behavioural approach
The psychodynamic approach
The evolutionary approach

Key concepts

Classical conditioning
- Association
- Stimulus and reflex response
- Unconditioned stimulus (UCS)
- Neutral stimulus (NS)
- Unconditioned reflex (UCR)
- Conditioned response (CR)
- Conditioned stimulus (CS)
- Forward conditioning
- Generalisation
- Discrimination
- One trial learning

Operant conditioning
- Reinforcement/rewards
- Punishments
- Aversive consequences
- Negative and positive reinforcers
- Primary reinforcers
- Shaping
- Reinforcement schedule
- Continuous reinforcement
- Extinguished
- Avoidance learning

Social learning theory
- Observation
- Indirect learning
- Role models
- Modelling
- Identification
- Vicarious reinforcement
- Expectancies of future outcomes
- Internal mental representations
- Direct reinforcement
- Value of the behaviour
- Self-efficacy

Strengths
- Concepts can be operationalised for more accurate manipulation and measurement.
- It is a falsifiable, empirical approach.
- The importance of rewards is supported by research (e.g. Lepper et al., 1973, found that children respond to rewards).
- It can account for individual differences in terms of selective reinforcement and context-dependent learning.

Limitations
- It relies on non-human animal evidence.
- At best it is a partial account.
- It does not explain effects of emotion, expectations, and higher level motivation on behaviour.
- It is a reductionist approach which prevents the investigation of other explanations and can never explain all behaviour.
- It is a determinist approach, which encourages lack of personal responsibility.

Strengths
- It includes effects of direct and indirect reinforcement.
- It involves cognitive factors in learning.
- It involves social influences (e.g. parents, media).
- It explains gender and cultural differences.

Limitations
- Other factors are also involved, e.g. genetic influences.
- Reinforcements are not sufficiently consistent to explain learning differences.

Methodology

Design decisions for a laboratory experiment
- Generate research aims
- Generate experimental hypothesis
- Operationalise IV and DV
- What design would be suitable?
- How should participants be selected?
- How will extraneous variables be controlled?
- What are the ethical issues?
- Is an ABAB design appropriate?

Strengths
- They can demonstrate causal relationships.
- Control of variables means high internal validity.
- Studies can be replicated, demonstrating reliability and validity.

Limitations
- They can be contrived and lack mundane realism.
- Operationalisation may reduce the meaningfulness of variables.
- Experimenter bias and demand characteristics can reduce internal validity.
- There may be ethical issues such as psychological harm because behaviour has changed.

Possible questions: see page vii

78

Chapter 11
Perspectives
Approaches >

The behavioural approach
The psychodynamic approach
The evolutionary approach

Key concepts

Effects of early experience on personality development

- Psychosexual stages
- Body parts
- Sexual (physical) stimulation
- Libido (psychic energy)
- Mouth (oral stage 0–18 months)
- Anus (anal stage 18 months–3 years)
- Genital region (phallic stage 3–6 years)
- Frustration or overindulgence may result in fixation
- Identification with one's same-sex parent
- Oedipus conflict
- Penis envy

Adult personalities

- The oral aggressive character is characterised by pessimism, envy and suspicion.
- The oral receptive character is optimistic, gullible and full of admiration for others.
- The anal retentive character is neat, stingy and obstinate.
- The anal expulsive character is disorganised, reckless and defiant.

Factors that motivate behaviour

- Id, ego and superego
- Pleasure principle
- Reality principle
- Conscious rational part
- Ego defence mechanisms (repression, displacement, reaction formation, intellectualisation)

Strengths

- It accounts for unconscious factors.
- It provides an account of the complexity of behaviour.
- There is support for ego defences, e.g. Williams' (1994) study of repression.
- There is support for the phallic stage, e.g. gender development theory (Martin and Halverson, 1981).
- There is support for rational versus irrational thinking, e.g. Solms' study (2000) on REM sleep.

Limitations

- It is difficult to falsify explanations.
- It is a determinist account, suggesting that certain behaviour is inevitable and beyond conscious control (determinism can also be a strength because causal relationships are revealed).
- It is gender-biased because it is based mainly on the male psyche.
- It is culture-biased because it is based on European women's accounts.
- Too much emphasis is placed on biological factors.
- Too little emphasis is placed on social influences.

Methodology

- Case studies

Strengths

- It provides rich details of individuals.
- It is not a reductionist approach but represents the complexity of life.
- It relates to real life.
- It is an idiographic approach, focusing on individuals rather than making generalisations which mask individual differences.
- Case studies can be collected together to make generalisations.

Other methods/techniques

- Psychoanalysis
- Free association
- Dream interpretation
- Manifest content
- Latent content
- Experiments

Limitations

- Unconscious reports cannot be validated.
- It is prone to researcher bias – the interviewer may affect answers given by interviewee.
- The interpretation of the therapist is subjective.
- It is difficult to generalise (idiographic).
- It is time-consuming and expensive.

Possible questions: see page vii

Chapter 11

Perspectives

Approaches   >

The behavioural approach

The psychodynamic approach

The evolutionary approach

Key concepts

Natural selection

- Selective pressure
- Fitness
- Adapted
- Environmental niche
- Survival
- Reproduction
- Genes, genetically transmitted

Sexual selection

- Exaggerated characteristics
- Males compete
- Females select
- Strategy
- Sexiest traits

Kin selection

- The selfish gene
- Inclusive fitness
- Gene pool
- The modular mind
- Ultimate
- Proximate
- Environment of evolutionary adaptation (EEA)
- Selection pressures
- Mental modules

Strengths

- It fits with genetic explanations; genes create vulnerabilities (i.e. predispose us to certain behaviours).
- It is not reductionist because it considers the function of behaviour.
- Ultimate functions are identified rather than proximate explanations.

Limitations

- It is reductionist – it reduces behaviour to adaptive significance in the EEA.
- It is determinist, suggesting that behaviour is inevitable and beyond our control.
- It ignores cultural influences.
- Speculative arguments are not supported by experimental evidence.

Methodology

Range of methods

- Naturalistic observations
- Experiments, mainly with non-human animals
- Surveys/interviews
- Cross-cultural studies

Strengths

- Observations are naturalistic: data that are collected are realistic and act as a starting point for a theory.
- Experiments: see behavioural approach.
- Surveys can collect a large quantity of data relatively easily, providing access to people's feelings and attitudes.
- Cross-cultural studies provide us with a less culturally biased view of human behaviour; therefore we are more likely to discover universals of human behaviour.

Limitations

- Naturalistic observation can't show cause and effect relationships; it is affected by observer bias and subject to ethical issues.
- Experiments: see behavioural approach.
- Surveys are prone to interviewer bias whereby the interviewer's behaviour may affect the interviewee's responses; interviewees are also prone to the social desirability bias when answering questions.
- Cross-cultural studies may be unrepresentative of the culture, employing imposed etics (use of methods designed for another culture) and prone to researcher bias.

Possible questions: see page vii